UNTAPPED TALENT

UNTAPPED TALENT

HOW SECOND CHANCE HIRING

WORKS FOR YOUR BUSINESS

AND THE COMMUNITY

JEFFREY D. KORZENIK

HarperCollins
LEADERSHIP

AN IMPRINT OF HarperCollins

Published by HarperCollins Leadership, an imprint of HarperCollins Focus LLC.

Any internet addresses, phone numbers, or company or product information printed in this book are offered as a resource and are not intended in any way to be or to imply an endorsement by HarperCollins Leadership, nor does HarperCollins Leadership vouch for the existence, content, or services of these sites, phone numbers, companies, or products beyond the life of this book.

ISBN 978-1-4002-2310-7 (eBook)
ISBN 978-1-4002-2314-5 (Paperback)

Library of Congress Control Number: 2020952624

Printed in the United States of America
21 22 23 LSC 10 9 8 7 6 5 4 3 2 1

Working with marginalized populations,
I meet so many who have nothing.

I have my family, so I have everything.
To my wife, Julie, and my sons, Andrew and James.

CONTENTS

A NOTE TO THE CURRENTLY INCARCERATED

IF YOU ARE READING THIS NOW, it means that you have gotten this book in a prison or jail library, or as a gift from a friend, family member, or a nonprofit that cares about your future. Thank you for taking the time to read it.

Since the day you entered prison or jail, you probably have felt that you are a burden. A burden to your family. A burden to your friends, to your community, to your country.

You are not a burden. You are a resource. As you'll read, our country is running out of the workforce we need to grow and prosper. The millions of people who, because of a criminal record, are not employed to the best of their potential are our best solution to this problem. This means you are a resource. A resource for your family. A resource for your friends, for your community, for your country. Not a burden.

You already know about the barriers you will face in getting a job after release. My hope is that this book will lower some of those hurdles and motivate employers to look beyond the mistakes and support the person ready to move forward.

Realize that employers, first and foremost, care about the character of the person they employ. The only thing they may know for sure about you is your mistake, and that it is an obstacle. You can help.

Whether through resources available in your facility or available after your release, demonstrate that you are not defined by your worst moment. If you need to work through challenges with emotional management and a personal history of trauma to rebuild yourself, embrace that opportunity. If you have battled addiction, keep fighting that good fight. If there are specific skills you can learn, learn them. If you do not have a high school diploma, work toward a GED. If you have an education, further it.

The fact that you are reading this book means that you are already educating yourself on the viewpoint and needs of employers.

The journey you must make is yours alone, although there will be friends, family, and allies to help.

Good luck and Godspeed.

PREFACE

THIS IS A BUSINESS BOOK about conventional business topics: talent acquisition, talent development, and risk mitigation. The argument for second chance hiring must stand alone as a business case to be sustainable and scalable. In the body of the book, I do not discuss the ethical case for second chance hiring, nor the implications for our society. However, those issues hover just beyond the pages of this book. As I finalize my manuscript in the summer of 2020, the nation has witnessed widespread protests that are fundamentally about the kind of society we want.

Like many people of my generation, in a business setting I am not comfortable discussing topics like social justice, racial justice, and systemic racism. When I use the language of earlier decades, it's much easier. I believe in giving people a fair shake, and that our country should offer opportunity for all, and I am vocal about this conviction. For me, the son and grandson of immigrants, the United States is where my parents and grandparents could start again, a land of second chances. I want that for others. We all do.

Equality of opportunity does not mean equality of outcomes, but one cannot escape the fact that the tens of millions of people with a criminal record don't get the same chance to succeed. That's unfair. We also know that, whatever brought us to this place, one in three

African American men in the United States has a felony conviction. It is hard to see how we can get to the kind of society we want when the burden of that kind of unfairness falls so disproportionately on one segment of our fellow citizens. Second chance hiring is not about addressing those ills, but it is a critical pathway to doing so. The path to a more equitable society must be paved by the business community.

When I set out to write this work, I had in mind a very different project. I have long been a fan of "creative nonfiction," factual books that read as if they are gripping fictional tales. My work, I imagined, would be a collection of the personal stories of pioneering business owners who offered employment to people in need of a second chance. I would share their life stories and deep personal convictions that led them to focus on the least among us, redeeming lives and communities in the wake of their work. These business owners are truly worthy of our admiration—when they took on the risk of hiring people with records, they took on personal financial risk, reputation risk, and even the potential loss of their employment and legacy. That's a lot of risk, and they have inspired me. While I mention many in passing, this work is not about them as individuals.

Many encouraged me to document the numerous beautiful narratives of personal redemption that are found among people with records. At so many gatherings on the topics of criminal justice reform and workforce development, these stories are highlighted, and my eyes are no drier than others in the room. The people who have made serious mistakes, paid for those mistakes, and rebuilt their lives to become different and better people are the unsung heroes of this book. So unsung, however, that not one of their journeys of personal redemption is featured in these pages.

At one point, I hoped to write the definitive compendium of every resource, law, and practice related to second chance hiring. While such a compilation would have enormous value, that's not the book I wrote either.

My career in researching and sharing insights on the economy and investment markets has allowed me to meet with and learn from tens of thousands of business owners and executives around the country. Their wisdom has given me unique insights into the US economy and has enhanced my career, but it also takes a lot of time. Prior to the coronavirus pandemic, I had flown on 125–150 flights annually for most of the last decade, spending a hundred nights a year in hotel rooms away from my family. The time limitations for an "outside" project like this book ultimately dictated that this work could not be any of the above, all-consuming, full-time projects, but I sincerely hope others take these on.

For years, I have been speaking about the subject matter of this book: the business case and best practices for hiring people with records. I was fairly confident that the arguments and especially the experiences of the business pioneers in this field were opening others to the possibility of second chance hiring. Two problems arose. One, I needed to better disseminate the knowledge I had collected— public speaking may be a catalyst for piquing the interest of the business community, but a forty-five-minute presentation just couldn't convey enough knowledge to support meaningful change. Two, I learned that those attendees who went back to their companies to investigate hiring people with records faced a wall of resistance. Even CEOs would get ground down by recalcitrant human resources directors, legal advisors, and CFOs. Those innovators willing to try second chance hiring deserved a guide and the opportunity to get the best results possible.

I offer one final note. Some encouraged me to make the moral case for giving second chances. I never felt I needed to do that. The business owners whom I have met, particularly those sitting at the pinnacle of their multi-decade careers who built tremendous businesses from the ground up, have shared one consistent concern with me: they want future generations of Americans to have the same opportunities to succeed that they had. It's hard to achieve that if people aren't given the opportunity to move beyond their past, and if they are always judged by their worst moments. Most people in the business community know that giving people a second chance is the right thing to do. The missing link has been a pathway to do this in a way that makes business sense. That was the book that was required. My fervent hope is that this work will meet that need.

JEFFREY D. KORZENIK
June 2020, Chicago, Illinois

INTRODUCTION

THE NEXT DECADE OF BUSINESS LEADERSHIP

What Will It Take
to Lead in the Decade Ahead?

The successful CEO of the future will be the one who can effectively manage through the coming talent shortage. That leader will understand the nature of this challenge, develop strategies to attract, develop, and retain a workforce, and inspire every level of company management to follow. This book will provide business leaders with an effective strategy for meeting this challenge.

Each economic cycle demands a different skill set that defines who will rise to the top in the business world. The successful CEOs of the 1970s navigated disruptive inflation and rising interest rates; the ability to control risk and exploit purchasing power drove success. The economist Thomas Mayer famously described the decade as the result of "the greatest failure of American macroeconomic policy in the postwar period."[1] The state of the nation was often measured by economist Arthur Okun's "misery index," which is the sum of the unemployment rate and inflation. For businesses, this meant uncertain consumer and input costs that varied widely. Oil prices quadrupled over the decade, while iron and steel prices nearly tripled. Risk management tools and pricing models that we take for granted today were adopted by the leaders of this period (see Figure 1).

Figure 1: The Misery Index

Those skills mattered less in the 1980s. As the misery index fell, confidence returned and effective leaders switched from the defense of the preceding decade to offense—building better and better products and services. Those who prospered did so by implementing total quality management, flattening their company hierarchies, and driving results through vision and mission statements. Readers of a certain age will be familiar with Sam Walton's famous ten rules[2] for building a business, rules that epitomized much of the formula for success in the 1980s. Four of "Mr. Sam's" rules revolve around breaking down the hierarchies that had dominated American management for a century. His view of employees as partners, focusing on their engagement, and his belief in sharing profits with workers, while considered common sense today, were pioneering in this period.

The 1990s brought forth new opportunities—and new management challenges—including broader and cheaper access to personal computer technology and the introduction of the internet for commercial use. The ability to lead through innovation defined the upper echelon of American business leadership as titans like Steve Jobs, Andy Grove, and Bill Gates became household names. Transformation was not found exclusively in the technology and telecom industries, as Jack Welch proved in his relentless focus on ensuring "upgrades" in his management ranks that were more powerful than many a software upgrade.

The history of our more recent decades is still being written, but some important characteristics of successful leadership have already been apparent. The 2000s required managers who could think internationally, whether through global sales or outsourcing to contain costs. The contribution of foreign earnings to the profits of the S&P 500 companies more than tripled in the years leading up to the Great Recession of 2007–2009. Even those who successfully navigated globalization might not have survived that financial crisis unless they also paid attention to strong balance sheets and access to credit.

The 2010 decade marked both the end and a new beginning of enormous significance, much of this relevant to the scope of this book. In a cycle with no major commercialized technological breakthroughs, extending the application of existing tools marked many business successes. For better or worse, crisis management and a Washington policy strategy became important additions to any leader's toolbox.

But leaders in this cycle have been faced with truly new and interrelated challenges: 1) the end of the period of rapid growth that had characterized the American economy since the end of World War II, 2) the (at least temporary) decline in productivity growth, and 3) the exit of baby boomers and entrance of millennials as the primary workers and significant consumers. Many of these factors are interrelated, but combined led to a severe labor and talent shortage.

As the 2010s came to a close, Labor Department statistics continued to show that job openings exceeded job-seekers. The National Federation of Independent Business (NFIB) surveys of small businesses cite the cost and availability of labor as the single biggest concern. Among larger companies, the CEOs and C-suite executives who participated in The Conference Board C-Suite Challenge 2019™ survey identified their primary internal challenge: attracting and retaining top talent. Strikingly, this was true not only in the United States, but across all regions of the world. Although this concern will be interrupted by recessions, the long-term challenge will not change. Without workers, you can't service your customers well. Without workers, you can't grow your business. And if your competitors can get workers when you can't, you lose.

It would be comforting to believe that this severe talent shortage is a mere cyclical concern, one that will dissipate with the next business cycle. It would be comforting to believe that this is a national problem that could be solved by global outsourcing. It would be comforting to believe that business leaders can ignore this challenge. But that would be wrong.

The pandemic of 2020 has elevated unemployment and freed workers, but even this has proven an incomplete solution for those companies that are still hiring. Yes, workers are available, but their skills and geography may not align with needs, retraining becomes less viable as workers age, and some workers are unavailable because of health concerns. To the degree that recessions create a surplus of available labor, it proves to be fleeting.

Demographics and Destiny

The world has had a traditional process for growing the workforce that adequately supplied business needs; it's called, "having children." Unfortunately, that is no longer enough.

The Canadian economist David Foot argues that demographics explains "two-thirds of everything."[3] From the perspective of this book, demographics will define 100 percent of the skills that business executives will need in the decade ahead. If the transition from a baby boomer to a millennial economy had "growing pains," that challenge will soon be dwarfed by the next demographic phase, one marked by a permanent shortage of labor. The United States, as well as the world, is simply not having many children. Birth rates reflect births in any given year and are subject to cyclical booms and busts. Following the millennials is one such bust—birth rates in the United States had a cyclical peak in 1990 and have declined since. Figure 2, from the World Bank, captures the story. Assuming that new full-time entrants to the workforce start in their early twenties, we already have a dwindling "supply" of early twenty-somethings relative to the overall population. Of course, immigration helps supply labor, but this is a factor that is secondary to US-born workers.

We might reasonably expect an improvement in the US birth rate as the large millennial generation enters childbearing years, but this will not tell the whole story. Demographers use the measurement of "fertility rate" to capture long-term population growth trends—the number of births a woman could expect over her total childbearing years. Simply to replace an existing population, excluding emigration and immigration, the fertility rate needs to be 2.1 in developed countries (the number is more than 2 to account for infant mortality).

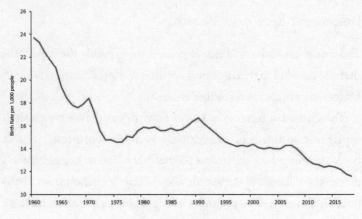

Figure 2: US Birth Rates

Even in those parts of the world with better fertility, most are not in the position to capitalize economically. Among mature economies, Israel is alone in having a fertility rate (3.1 in 2017) that exceeds the replacement rate but is too small to meaningfully impact global labor force demand. Among large emerging economies, China's fertility rate is a paltry 1.6, and while India still exceeds the replacement rate, the trend is distinctly negative. The vast majority of countries that have robust fertility rates are too far behind in economic development and thus not in a position to provide outsourced labor solutions.

What should leaders take away from this blizzard of statistics? The bottom line is that our current labor shortage is not going to pass. Over the longer term, it is likely to get worse. If today the lack of workers is a major irritant; in the decade ahead, for businesses that do not address this challenge, it will represent an existential threat.

The Next New Skill

When December 31, 2029, ends, what essential skills will define business leadership in the 2020s? The demographic challenge argues that those skills must revolve around the ability to attract and retain a productive labor force. The days are already past when accommodations of business casual or a Ping-Pong table in the break room are sufficient. The next-generation leader will have to dig deeper into untapped talent pools. This will require experimentation, flexibility, and creativity not always associated with staffing functions. Fortunately, aspiring leaders can learn today from pioneers, who have already developed models of success. This book is the summation of the work of those pioneers, who have found a deep and broad talent pool in the unlikeliest places.

UNTAPPED TALENT

1

THE HEART OF GROWTH

I've got some bad news: growing your business is going to get harder in the decades ahead. You may have already experienced difficulty in finding enough employees to fill all available jobs; that difficulty is going to get worse. And, unfortunately, falling birth rates don't just mean that workers will be harder to find—consumers will become harder to find, too, and the economy will grow more slowly. A slower-growth economy is a more vulnerable economy, with higher uncertainty and risks.

Over the next two chapters, I will show you the size of the problem we face. And then, over the rest of the book, I will explain the solution you and your business should consider.

First, some basic economics to put our situation in perspective. The potential for any nation's economy to grow boils down to two factors: 1) How fast can it grow its employed labor force, and 2) how quickly can it grow the productivity of its workers. The product of this sum is the long-term growth *potential*.

The concept of growth potential only plays out over the course of an economic cycle and rarely defines the actual growth rate in a single year. In recessions, growth is far below potential, and in the early years of recoveries, growth tends to exceed that limit as employers start to take up the slack from the previous downturn. It is only in the final period of growth in a cycle, as the economy pushes against full employment, that the potential growth rate is more likely to align with actual growth. Changes in workforce size and productivity are the twin throttles that dictate long-term growth, even if this is not apparent in any given year.

Figure 3, with data produced by the Congressional Budget Office (CBO), shows both historic and projected gross domestic product (GDP) growth in the modern US economy in terms of workforce (the dark gray bars) and productivity (the light gray bars). Many important social trends are captured in these statistics: the post–World War II shift to a consumer economy, the growth of the number of working women, and the growth of the internet, to name but a few.

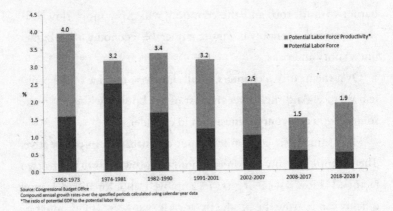

Figure 3: US Potential GDP Growth

Fifty years ago, our grandparents enjoyed GDP growth of, on average, close to 4 percent. In fact, growth only slightly lower than this, and over 3 percent, continued until 2001. The post-2007 hangover resulted in only 1.5 percent average growth for almost a decade.[1]

Whatever the trends of the past, the CBO calculations point to this future—US potential growth is slowing and projected to be just below 2 percent.[2] This trend extends a historically low era of growth. Two questions arise in response: "Why?" and "What can we do?"

Productivity Considerations

One answer has to do with productivity.

The natural business response to a tougher environment is, "How can we do more with less?" Economists call that *productivity*, and it is an important driver of profits and even societal wealth. Productivity growth should be part of every business's strategy, but achieving those benefits can be costly or outside a leader's control. The focus of this book is not on the productivity component of potential growth, but rather on the dynamics of our labor force. However, for the sake of completeness, it is important to understand the nature of productivity growth and where it intersects with our emphasis on workforce strategies.

At its most basic, productivity is our GDP divided by hours worked. While hours worked is a fairly straightforward concept, GDP is far more complex. The accepted definition of GDP is the total value of final goods and services adjusted by our net exports in a given year. While simple in concept, the "value" ascribed to many goods is not simply the price; it also involves arcane adjustments for quality and technological advancements.

The calculation of GDP is not a complete measure of other things we might value. While it would include the purchase of environmental control equipment, for example, it does not measure a cleaner environment. Even in the measurement of material goods, value calculations do not capture what economists call "consumer surplus," benefits consumers derive without having to pay more (think of all the flavor choices you have at the ice cream parlor that cost no more than the vanilla cone). Despite these concerns, GDP and productivity are highly representative of what is going on in the economy, with productivity being the multiplier factor, taking worker hours and turning them into goods and services valued by others.

Accepting GDP at face value, what factors drive greater production of goods and services for each hour worked? The single most important *short-term* driver of productivity growth is capital investment—traditionally land, buildings, and machinery, which most certainly includes software and other technology. Many of these investments require large initial outlays and long payback periods, requiring high levels of confidence and access to financing. Because confidence and financing have cyclical characteristics, such investments come and go. In general, sluggish productivity growth in the United States in the past decade can be attributed to weak investment and aged capital stock. The good news for businesses today is that, for those who are willing and able to invest, updating old equipment provides outsized returns.

Innovation also plays an important role in productivity growth. The United States has long been fertile territory. High levels of entrepreneurship, strong commercialization of academic research, and a robust venture capital ecosystem all help support productivity growth, but none of these strengths should be taken for granted.

Finally—and most important for this book—there is a human element to productivity growth. Providing workers with education and training can lift productivity. Even demographic factors can play a role. Workers in their thirties and early forties go through a rapid acquisition of new skills, experience, and career commitment that are associated with higher productivity, evidenced by their ability to earn much higher levels of compensation—the biggest jump in adult pay occurs during these years. The millennial generation, the largest component of our workforce, may provide a meaningful boost to US productivity growth in the years ahead.

Hiring, training, and retaining workers will become the most critical steps the business leaders of the future can take to increase productivity.

Measuring Our Workforce Potential

The best solution to a nationwide growth challenge is found in human capital—more and better workers. Fortunately, a low unemployment rate doesn't mean our labor force is tapped out, and wise leaders can exploit this potential. But first they have to understand it.

We know from the discussion of birth and fertility rates in the Introduction that the growth of the size of the working-age population will become increasingly constrained. This assumes, of course, no change to our immigration policies; given dwindling fertility rates abroad, even immigration may not offer an easy solution.

Birth and fertility rates are drivers of the size of the *future* working-age populace. Our initial formulation that potential growth is dictated by productivity growth and workforce growth suggests that working-age population is an insufficient measure—we must also incorporate the degree to which this group is "in the game" and ready to be employed. To measure our efficiency in tapping today's labor pool, economists use a metric called *labor force participation rate*. This is defined as the percentage of noninstitutionalized civilians age sixteen and older who are either working or actively seeking employment. The Federal Bureau of Labor Statistics, an arm of the Department of Labor, is the definitive source of this data. Figure 4 shows the history of this metric since 1948.

Figure 4: US Labor Force Participation Rate

It should come as no surprise that our greatest decades of rising labor force participation, the 1980s and 1990s, were also among our strongest years of GDP growth.[3] Those decades included two large and beneficial trends—the entrance of the baby boomer generation into the workforce and rapidly rising rates of female participation in the labor force. When we utilize an ever-greater percent of our population in the production of goods and services, we benefit.

Conversely, the falling labor force participation rate since 2000 is linked to the generally lackluster rates of growth. Once again, demographics are a big part of the story. The denominator of the labor force participation rate has no age limit; thirty-year-old and hundred-year-old people are assessed alike in calculating this metric. When a growing percentage of our adult population exceeds retirement age, everything else being equal, the labor force participation rate will fall. In 2001, the oldest of the baby boom generation (those born between 1946 and 1964) turned fifty-five. At this age, retirement becomes increasingly likely, and more than half of workers age sixty-two have already left the workforce. Given the impact of retirement on labor force participation and the massive size of the baby boomer demographic, it's natural that participation rates would decline.

But not that much. In fact, not even *close* to that much. There's a "missing" labor force—a missing segment of our population absent from the workplace and causing labor force participation rates to fall well below what would be expected.

The successful business leader is the one who can reframe "missing" as "hidden potential."

Full Employment and the Current Gap

About 160 million civilians (technically, nonfarm civilian workers) are working in the United States.[4] (For ease of explanation and because our economy is constantly changing, I'll use big, round numbers.) The most important measure, and the one associated with growth, is the annual change in that number.

The economic expansion that began in 2009 has added about 2.5 million workers each year to grow at the roughly 2 percent annual pace that has characterized the business cycle that only ended with the 2020 COVID-19 pandemic. Given that this rate of growth is close to the long-term assessment of US growth projected by the CBO, that 2.5 million annual addition of workers is a very good estimate of average future needs as well.

Where did these new workers come from?

Some came from other employers. There is "churn" in the labor markets, with employers finding workers already employed by others. But economic growth rests on the net additions to the payrolls, and thus our ultimate interest is in the employment of those without a job. So, other than other employers, where do new employees come from?

In times of higher unemployment, generally during the down period of an economic cycle, employers can fill many of their needs by sourcing from the ranks of unemployed job-seekers. In an environment with an unemployment rate of 6 percent or more, hiring managers can often find candidates with strong experience, requisite skills, and perhaps someone with whom they have a personal connection.

Employers also rely on new additions to the workforce. New additions are one of two things: immigrants or new adults. In any given year, between 1 and 1.5 million new workers come from immigration and natural growth of the working-age population. That immigration number includes programs like the H1B visa (85,000 granted each year), legal immigrants, and (to use as neutral a term as possible) unauthorized immigrants. The natural growth of the native-born, working-age population is the most significant component of new workers, by far—but the fact that the birth rate started to decline a generation ago suggests that this is already becoming a less fruitful resource.[5]

If growth progresses at a sufficient pace, "full employment" is achieved. This is not when the unemployment rate reaches zero, but rather when labor resources are so efficiently used that the only remaining unemployment is the result of natural friction. There's always some small level of people between jobs, facing structural barriers, or enjoying voluntary periods without work. Although different in each cycle, post–World War II historic lows in US unemployment give us a sense of where the lowest bound may be: 2.5 percent in 1954, 3.4 percent in 1969, 3.9 percent in 2000.[6]

Whenever that lower bound to unemployment approaches, the US economy becomes at a very real risk of running out of room to grow. This usually resolves as a tight labor market drives wages higher, well past the point they can be offset by productivity, in turn driving inflation beyond tolerable limits, and thus leading to higher interest rates (either driven by markets or central bankers), which choke off growth, ending the business cycle.

Once full employment is reached, the annual shortfall of workers is simply the difference between annual growth needs and the number of new workers from immigration and new adults.

We were at one of these points in the final quarters of the 2009–2020 economic expansion—technically full employment. We can quantify our annual shortfall of workers faced by US businesses—it's the difference between our annual increase in labor needs (about 2.5 million workers) and the number produced by immigration and demographic forces (1–1.5 million).

In other words, we were currently falling short by at least a million workers each year, and demographics dictate that we'll get there again. While the expansion of 2009–2020 may be over, understanding worker shortage cycles will be critical to solving the coming expansion's shortfall.

▶ ▶ ▶

Measuring the Missing

This then becomes the scale of our challenge: short a million-plus workers for each year of economic growth once the unemployment rate hits bottom.[7]

This is potentially disastrous. An economy that has too few workers to grow at a robust pace is more than just a slower-growing economy. It is an economy forever teetering on the edge of a recession. It is an economy that limits access to credit. It is an economy that does not engender the optimism to invest in training and productivity improvements that build societal wealth. And, as we are seeing in global political movements, slow-growing economies undermine confidence in capitalism, trade, and free societies.

This Time Is Different: Three Social Ills and the Labor Market

When adjusting for the age and sex of the US population, only about half of the decline in labor force participation can be explained. A solid two to three million Americans appear to be "missing." This equates to a shortfall that could have provided the labor fuel for several more years of growth, or for far faster growth or some combination of longer and stronger. Even as we move beyond the economic downturn of the pandemic, a depressed labor force participation rate will slow and limit our potential. We must understand this loss to American economic vitality if we are to have any chance of restoring our labor markets to their historic strength and address the long-term problem for employers of finding workers.

Who are these "missing workers"? And is there a way to identify them and bring them back into the workforce?

It turns out we can identify, generally, who these missing workers are and where they went. They fall into three broad categories. Specifically, three social ills, present today in ways wholly unlike past economic cycles, have suppressed labor force participation rates: long-term unemployment, the opioid epidemic, and the incarceration/recidivism cycle. Of course, social ills are always present, but actually applying a quantitative analysis to contemporary problems argues that the magnitude and dispersion of today's societal challenges represent not a difference of degree, but a difference of kind.

You would have to go back to the Great Depression to find comparable long-term unemployment; back to the influenza pandemic of 1918 to find a health issue with the same impact on the workforce as opioids today; and you would find that there is no precedent in US history for the labor implications of our incarceration/recidivism cycle. We'll review each of these social ills and show that they individually have robbed the American economy of hundreds of thousands of workers and, when combined, deplete us of millions.

A running joke I learned long ago on Wall Street goes like this:

What are the most dangerous words in skiing? "Follow me, Dad!"

What are the most dangerous words in investing? "This time, it's different!"

Economic cycles tend to look alike. Even seemingly anomalous downturns like the Great Recession of 2007–2009 had their precedent in the "financial panics" of the early twentieth century and numerous similar threats to the entire financial system that befell the nineteenth century. So it is a bold statement indeed to claim there is anything particularly new about any given economic cycle. Yet, that's the inescapable conclusion of an examination of the data.

One of the easiest ways to visualize this departure from the past is to examine the statistics that measure the first of our labor force–sapping problems: the persistence of long-term unemployment. The standard definition of "long-term unemployment" is fulfilled when joblessness persists twenty-seven consecutive weeks or longer (past the half-year mark). Short-term unemployment is a commonplace occurrence in the US economy, but long-term unemployment is less common and far more destructive. The long-term unemployed have far greater difficulty reentering the workforce than those unemployed for only a short period, and the problem worsens the longer the duration of unemployment.

There are some underlying reasons that long-term unemployment is detrimental to job-seekers. Those in the tech industry may find their skills become obsolete, while those in physically demanding positions may simply find that a period of absences degrades their fitness. It is unfortunate that those who return to work after long-term unemployment often do not fare well and become unemployed again. Whether it is this track record or simple prejudice, employers often actively avoid considering those who have been unemployed for a long period of time.[8]

Figure 5 shows just how abnormal was the impact of the Great Recession. This graph displays the average duration of unemployment in the United States going back to 1948: after someone leaves a job (involuntarily or voluntarily, how long, on average, before they are reemployed), the average period of unemployment fluctuates with economic conditions. In booming economic times, this is relatively short, roughly ten weeks. If a worker loses a job in a recession, however, it takes longer to gain new work—*but it is critical to observe just how much longer.* In past cycles, that average duration rarely got beyond twenty weeks. In the aftermath of the Great Recession, the average—*average*—period between jobs ballooned to double that number. By April 2010, 6.8 million Americans had been unemployed for twenty-seven weeks or longer, more than 45 percent of all unemployed job-seekers, and in July 2011, the average duration of unemployment peaked at 40.7 weeks.[9]

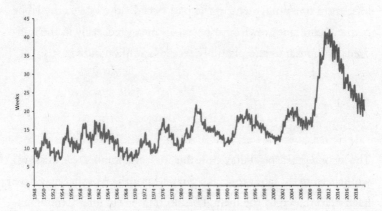

Figure 5: Average Duration of Unemployment

Keep in mind that this is an arithmetic (mean average), with many job-seekers unemployed for more than a year. In fact, the official government scorekeeper of these measures, the Bureau of Labor Statistics (BLS), observed that by the end of 2010, 11 percent of the unemployed had been unemployed for more than two full years, and changed its data collection to allow reporting of unemployment durations as long as five years.

The costs of such long-term unemployment are considerable. Known impacts are long-term earnings losses, career volatility, the physical and mental health of the individual, and even the educational outcomes for their children. For our purposes, though, the key outcome is that many of the long-term unemployed simply drop out of the labor force. The longer the duration of unemployment, the more likely that the worker simply drops out, lowering the labor force participation rate. Economists Alan Krueger, Judd Cramer, and David Cho examined joblessness from 2008 to 2012 and calculated that roughly half of those who had been unemployed for eighteen months simply left the labor force altogether. Given the millions experiencing long-term unemployment in the past decade, the loss to the labor market—and our growth prospects—is measured easily in the hundreds of thousands and plausibly exceeds a million individuals.

The Opioid Epidemic: Where Tragedy and Economics Meet

The second great social ill responsible for large numbers of "missing" workers from the labor force is a physical health crisis that may have been exacerbated by the mental health burdens of long-term unemployment. I'm speaking, of course, about the opioid epidemic. Self-medication through opioid use was but one part of a complex narrative that resulted in both a societal tragedy and an economic burden. The numbers are truly shocking. The nearby graph compares drug overdose deaths to many other well-known causes of premature deaths. The US government estimates that more than 72,000 people in the country died of overdoses in 2017, and more than two-thirds were opioid-related. That's more than all the American soldiers lost in the Vietnam War, more than the peak of the HIV/AIDS epidemic, more than gun homicides. The toll exceeds those from car crashes, a number that itself includes deaths in which opioid and other drug intoxication played a role. In other words, we should understand that the drug epidemic is so severe that it represents a historical anomaly ("this time, it's different"). Looking beyond the tragic death toll reveals this scourge to be not just a societal disaster, but an economic one as well (see Figure 6).

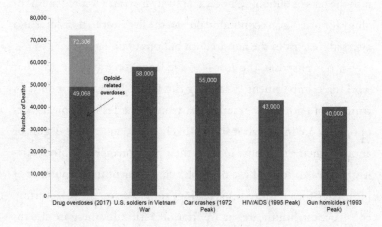

Figure 6: The Opioid Tragedy

Opioid and other drug-related overdoses are a terrible tragedy, a waste of lives (often young). What makes this all the more poignant is the knowledge that nearly a quarter of those who became addicted started innocently with a doctor's prescription. Yet, from the standpoint of the impact on the labor force, these tens of thousands of deaths are just the tip of the iceberg. The US Department of Health and Human Services (HHS) estimates that the number of people using opioids for non-medicinal purposes is 11.5 million. Amazingly, this is actually an improvement from the peak usage of 12.5 million in 2015, but still astoundingly high so many years into a recognized health crisis. HHS estimates that the total number of those we might think of as "addicts," those who fit the definition of opioid use disorder, exceeds two million people.

The economic cost of opioid abuse is difficult to measure. The direct cost of treatment measures in the billions of dollars each year. Studies that weigh broader economic costs, including crime and incarceration related to the opioid epidemic, assess the annual toll well into the tens of billions. One federal study used an accepted methodology for placing an economic value on the lives lost to overdoses and assessed the cost in the hundreds of billions of dollars.[10]

For our purposes, the cost is to the labor force and the way that workforce impairment is sapping the vitality of the economy. In truth, we do not know exactly how many of the 11.5 million abusers of opioids are in the labor force—likely many, and to one degree or another, their drug abuse impairs their performance and productivity. Even casual opioid use precludes employment in any number of industries that require drug testing, for example, manufacturing, construction, healthcare, transportation. Critically, these are also industries that offer paths to well-compensated employment for those without traditional four-year college degrees.

Of the 2.1 million estimated addicts (opioid use disorder), a large number are not in the labor force. Given our tragic overdose death statistics, the path for many is not merely leaving the workforce, but loss of life. Opioid addiction at this level is associated with other behaviors that impede employment: criminal activity, loss of housing stability, and health issues that go well beyond the behavioral impairment of the drug abuse.

The late economist Alan Krueger studied the impact of opioid use on the labor force. In a series of studies, his work suggested that a significant decline in the labor force participation rate was related to the opioid epidemic. Notably, he concluded in his paper that 43 percent of the decline in male participation rates and 25 percent of the decline in female labor force participation rates from 1999 to

2015 could be associated with opioid prescription, observing, "Nearly half of prime age NLF [Not in the Labor Force] men take pain medication on a daily basis, and in nearly two-thirds of these cases they take prescription pain medication. Labor force participation has fallen more in areas where relatively more opioid pain medication is prescribed, causing the problem of depressed labor force participation and the opioid crisis to become intertwined." In related calculations, Krueger points to heavy drug use not being a medical necessity, as geographic variations in drug use are related to policies rather than population health.[11] Moreover, his survey work may actually underestimate the problem, since the truly addicted or illicit users are less likely to be respondents or to answer honestly. Even so, his work suggests that we are missing several million workers due to opioid abuse.

It Gets Worse: The Biggest Barrier to Workforce Participation

If the despair of long-term unemployment could be a factor in the opioid epidemic, the abuse and trade in opioids is most certainly a contributing factor to our third exceptional contributor to declining labor force participation: the US incarceration and recidivism cycle. While drug-related crime has accelerated this social challenge, it predates the opioid crisis.

There are so many ways that our experience in this area is exceptional (and not in a good sense). Let's start with international comparisons. According to the Institute of Criminal Policy Research at the University of London, the United States is a world leader in its incarcerated population rate, the percentage of the population that is currently held in prison, jails, and other correctional facilities.

In fairness, these comparisons do not include the sizeable numbers held in nontraditional detention in authoritarian regimes like China and North Korea, but it is safe to say our use of incarceration far exceeds any developed country. We also have very limited data on the international comparison of jails to prisons (jails are generally used for pretrial detention and for very short periods of incarceration administered by local officials, as opposed to longer sentences for felonies in state and federal facilities). The Prison Policy Initiative points out that jails have an extraordinarily high "churn." Although their work indicates that some six hundred thousand people are held in jails in the United States at any given time, there are more than ten million admissions to jails each year, some the same individuals, but clearly a very high number.

We should also understand that US incarceration rates have not always been this high. As Figure 7 illustrates, we went through an unusual period of growth of our state and federal prison population, particularly in the 1990s, that has left us where we are today.

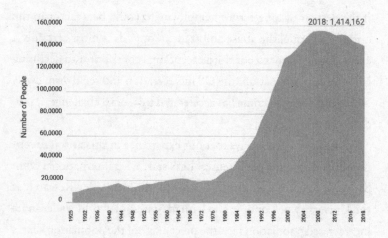

Figure 7: US State and Federal Prison Population 1925–2018

The impact extends far beyond the statistics of those in prisons. We should acknowledge that the increase in incarceration at the community level had very different impacts. Figure 8 displays the percentage of the population with prison records by state. The darker the shading, the greater the intensity of prison records within the community. The top row compares that measure for the total population to that of the African American population in 1980, before the big ramp-up in incarceration began. The bottom row shows this measure after three decades of rising incarceration. It becomes immediately apparent that the African American community has felt this change most intensely.

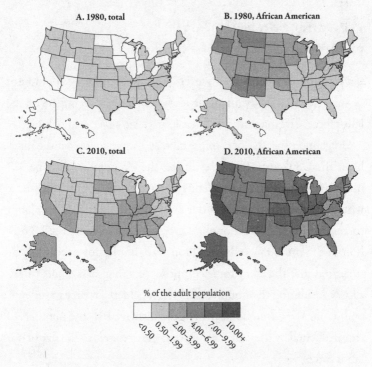

Percentage of US adult population with prison records by state and race, 1980–2010

Figure 8: Disparate Impact of Incarceration

It is far beyond the purview of this book to discuss broad criminal justice, policing, and sentencing reform (although in Chapter Seven I'll suggest a few changes that could positively impact both public safety and economic outcomes). There are many areas in which Americans of goodwill can simply disagree. Our concern is the objective impact of the criminal justice system on the workforce.[12]

What exactly has been the impact of our exceptional period of incarceration on the workforce? The answer revolves around what happens after incarceration, or indeed any time a potential worker carries a criminal record.

The Labor Force Aftermath of Incarceration and Recidivism

Given our exceptionally high levels of incarceration, we should not be surprised that the criminal justice system has had an impact on the labor force. The magnitude of that impact, however, is shocking.

To gain perspective, it is important, as always, to look at the numbers. The US Census Bureau estimates the US population to be 327 million (2018). The broadly defined "working age population," those who are ages fifteen to sixty-four, is 206 million. The civilian labor force, the focus of the economic concerns (i.e., excluding the 1.3 million in the military), is 163 million. We should not necessarily be surprised that the labor force comprises less than half of all Americans, considering the number of children, elderly, retirees, students, and so on. We *should* be surprised, and dismayed, by the numbers of those touched by the criminal justice system relative to the size of our labor force.

Figure 9 tallies the number of people who have been touched by the criminal justice system in a way that could adversely impact labor force participation and employment. This ranges from the 2.3 million who are incarcerated or under supervision (typically post-incarceration parole) to the widely cited 70 million (typically mischaracterized as "one in three adults in the United States have a criminal record").[13]

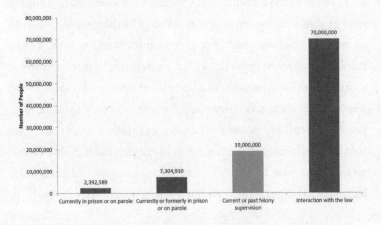

Figure 9: Criminal Justice Impact

It is worth understanding what each of these statistics represents. To start, the terms *probation* and *parole* are sometimes used interchangeably, but they have different definitions. *Parole* is supervision after release from prison; it is ordered by parole boards or by statute. *Probation* is a type of supervision that is often used in lieu of imprisonment or sometimes as part of a "split sentence," with the court ordering time both incarcerated and on probation at time of sentencing. In both instances, failure to comply with the terms of supervision can result in (further) incarceration. With regard to these statistics, someone who has been on parole has also been incarcerated, but someone who has been under felony supervision might have been on probation and never incarcerated.

All the distinctions matter from the standpoint of workforce impact. Clearly, those incarcerated, with a very small number of exceptions through work-release programs, are not contributing to the economy—they are not even included in the calculation of labor force participation rates.

Those who have been incarcerated have a particularly difficult time gaining employment—a Prison Policy Initiative study found an estimated 27 percent were unemployed, more than five times a comparable group in the general population. Beyond those serving prison sentences, those who have not been convicted but are part of the huge population churning through jails for temporary, short-term, or pretrial detention have at a minimum a period of work disruption that impairs long-term employment. In general, those with incarceration in their past are not only less likely to be employed but are also less likely to have stability in any employment that they do land.

"WHAT DO I CALL YOU?"

Among some criminal justice advocates, there is an active effort to change the language used to describe people with criminal records. This is a laudable effort to help reframe dialogue, particularly when done in a supportive and inclusive manner (like the efforts of Dawn Freeman and the Securus Foundation "Language Matters" campaign). In the hands of some activists, however, it can become scolding and get in the way of important conversations. Even when technically correct, terms like "felon" tend to be frowned upon and "ex-offender" is not embraced, with preference for tongue-twisters like "justice-involved individuals" or "returning citizens" or "second chancers." I've had well-meaning people take issue with each of these terms, so it sometimes feels like there is no winning. "People with records" seems to be widely accepted and is frequently used in this book. Regardless, these language disputes shouldn't get in the way of serious and respectful discussion.

I like to share a story told to me by Pete Leonard, the founder and CEO of Second Chance Coffee Roasters. Doing business as I Have a Bean, he built a coffee roaster staffed largely by people with criminal records. Not only has he had tremendous success helping people rebuild their lives, but he operates a profitable business that produces the best coffee I've ever tasted (find out for yourself: www.ihaveabean.com). Each bag is proudly signed by the employee who roasted the finished product.

When he first gathered his team to build his business, Pete shared with me that he asked his employees, "What do I call you?"

They responded unanimously, "Oh, we're 'felons.' Just use our names when you address us individually."

Any touch with the criminal justice system can be an obstacle to employment. The broadest measure of those who have interacted with this system is seventy million. This number is derived by taking the number of individuals whose names appear in state criminal databases and reducing it by an assumption that some individuals appear in the records of multiple states. The problem with this approach is that state criminal databases may include records, depending on the state, for traffic violations, tax liens, and other legal issues that are civil and not criminal matters. These records also include people who were charged with crimes but are innocent in the eyes of the law— either by having those charges dismissed, by not adjudicating, or by being found not guilty. There is indeed some truth that such records can cause employment issues. Many misdemeanors would give an employer pause, and a mug shot of someone ultimately found innocent may appear in a background check. Still, the seventy million is an overly broad number and does not represent the labor force impact of the incarceration and recidivism cycle in the American economy. A clear barrier to employment faces the nineteen million Americans who have a felony conviction, and we are on firm ground in recognizing this number in our examination of national workforce issues. Of that nineteen million, more than ten million have no history of prison incarceration, but nonetheless have a felony record (and may have faced some combination of short time in county jails, fines or community service). Even without the disruption of incarceration, a felony record is a significant barrier to employment.[14]

There are, of course, regulatory restrictions to employing people with records, particularly felonies, but misdemeanors as well. Some of these limitations are widely accepted as sensible public-safety precautions, but many are overreaching. The restrictions placed on people with a criminal conviction are broadly known as "collateral sanctions." The National Inventory of Collateral Consequences of Convictions, a project developed by the American Bar Association and now administered by the Council of State Governments Justice Center, has identified roughly 45,000 such barriers to employment, housing, education, and other opportunities. Of most direct relevance to the workforce are occupational licensing restrictions, but even tangential hurdles can impact the ability of someone with a criminal conviction to stay employed (e.g., lack of access to housing). While some states have a process to grant exemptions to some of these barriers, significant government-imposed obstacles remain.

The biggest obstacle to employment for a person with a criminal record is simply the inability even to be considered by a hiring company. In an age of electronic applications, when entry-level jobs can attract hundreds of résumés, employers increasingly rely on algorithms to narrow the pool. Whether through automated Applicant Tracking Systems or through company rules, someone with a criminal record is typically excluded from even initial consideration. In places where "ban the Box" legislation does not allow for this initial filtering, there is evidence to suggest that some employers may be utilizing proxy screens to avoid candidates with criminal records.

The biggest reason, however, that employers do not want to consider people with criminal records is conscious choice. Some consider a criminal record to be evidence of critical character flaws. Some associate someone who has a record with high potential for violence or workplace theft. Even among those who tried hiring from this pool, they found success too random—some were great employees and some were terrible; the reality of management is that the burdens of one bad employee outweigh the benefits of several good ones, so random success wasn't viable.

Where's the Labor Opportunity?

Our deepest and broadest labor opportunity comes from the ranks of those underemployed because of a criminal record.

Of course, there are opportunities in those who have left after long-term unemployment, those who struggle with addiction, and various permutations of all our social ills. But the employers who have succeeded in employing marginalized workers largely target those with criminal records and have built processes that address the issues that come with this population.

The successful businesses that have informed the best practices that this book will share don't discriminate—they provide opportunities to recovering addicts, those left behind by the Great Recession, and those struggling with any number of other life issues preventing past participation in the labor force. Many of those sidelined through long-term unemployment were sidelined a decade ago, and between time away and aging out of the workforce, this pool may no longer be available. Certainly, employers who automatically exclude the long-term unemployed candidates from consideration may want to rethink this filter, but that is different from a proactive strategy. There are also some very interesting initiatives in corporate America to attract women (and some men) who have left the workforce to raise families. Rising female labor force participation rates have been one of the true bright spots in the US workforce. Employers are increasingly willing to work with existing employees who have tested positive on drug tests. However, while opioid use is widespread, the number of those who are unemployed because of use is relatively small, and of those, the number who are on an effective road to recovery may be smaller still. There is also a strong relationship between addiction and criminal records, so in many ways, these pools overlap.

But the biggest resource is those with a criminal record who are either unemployed or underemployed.

To be clear, this group's unemployment is not driven by lack of desire to work—according to the Prison Policy Initiative, labor force participation (which includes job hunting, not just actual employment) is above the demographic peer group. To get a sense of the size of this pool, we consider the nineteen million people with felony records as the group most likely to be *under*employed (either unemployed or not given the opportunity to perform to their economic potential). Of those, more than sixteen million are outside of incarceration. Of those, probably ten to twelve million are still of working age. Many are undoubtedly employed, but given the significant obstacles to their employment, many of these could be employed at a higher level. The talent pool of any group this size is also diverse—it includes people with advanced professional degrees as well as people experienced in the trades, and it increasingly includes people receiving industry certifications and industry-driven training within prisons.

RAY DALTON: THE ENTREPRENEUR

Perhaps better than anyone I've met, Ray Dalton embodies the opportunity and potential for second chance hiring. Ray is a second chance employer, a successful business leader, an innovator in both business and charity, and someone who himself was given a second chance. His life demonstrates that people can move beyond their youthful mistakes. His company shows the viability of employing people with records and the model for doing so. His entrepreneurship supports the thesis that innovators in hiring are innovators in business. His charitable work reveals the power of bringing business acumen to solving social ills like reentry.

Raised in a foster home in some of the toughest neighborhoods in Los Angeles, the overriding rule of the house, to ensure government foster checks would continue to arrive, was "Don't get caught." A reflection of his challenged upbringing, but perhaps also revealing a glimmer of the future entrepreneur, Ray and his brother would shoplift wine and cigarettes to sell to people on the street on the way to school so they would have money to buy lunch. Eventually, at age seventeen, he dropped out of high school, went to night school to learn auto mechanics, and settled into "life." It was at that time, faced with a difficult life decision, that Ray enlisted in the US Air Force. The structure and opportunities offered would profoundly change the course of Ray's life.

There are few businessmen who could claim greater success than Ray Dalton. The year before we met, he had sold the ninth business he had founded, PartsSource, and still had several other successful ventures. When PartsSource was sold, it was already established as a leading e-commerce supplier in the medical device equipment industry, described to me as the "Amazon of parts" in its field, facilitating 1.5 million transactions each year and supplying more than three thousand hospitals worldwide.

The story of Ray's life could be a compelling variation on a rags-to-riches tale. But this is not about Ray's life, rather the life that he has given to others. Motivated by his own experience and his deep Christian faith, roughly a quarter of his employees have been second chance hires, people with criminal records. Like other employers in this book, Ray learned that employment was not enough, and he takes a deep interest in coaching and accountability for his second chance hires. He also provides, directly or through referrals, many of the social services that people with criminal records often need to support continued employment. After a good employee was returned to prison on a technical violation related to unpaid traffic and parking tickets from years prior, Ray established a fund to lend employees the money (interest free) to clear up any of the legal obligations that could be barriers to their reentry.

His extensive charitable work includes a family foundation, but of particular relevance is reLink.org, a separate nonprofit that developed and supports a cell phone–friendly internet site that provides local resources for housing, food, addiction treatment, or any of the other hurdles that can block the successful reentry of people with records or other marginalized workers. The site relink.org is a tool not only for the challenged employee, but also for those interested in the welfare of that employee: social workers, human resources professionals, and supervisors. Ray also argues that the site's data

> collection potential makes relink.org an effective tool for governments looking to understand how these community resources are used and how financial support might best be deployed.

Employers who hire second chance workers have access to a labor pool overlooked by competitors and community partners who are willing to help them staff and train employees. Some of that support includes financial incentives, but while these can be helpful, no incentive can make up for a bad employee. What we will espouse in coming chapters are the tools for finding and supporting employees who are so good that you don't need a tax incentive. This is not charity, this is business. Best of all, these are not pie-in-the-sky theoretical models developed in an ivory tower. Everything I have learned has been through the experiences of for-profit business owners who have pioneered this type of staffing and have generously shared their processes.

The Costs of Inaction

Before we delve into the successful models of second chance hiring, we should weigh those benefits against the cost of inaction. Inaction at the business level means that staffing challenges will only get worse as the postmillennial birth rate declines, the baby boomers increasingly retire, and some millennial workers leave to raise families. Staffing costs will rise, crimping profit margins and causing more reliance on automation, a long-term commitment with uncertain payoff. Businesses will increasingly play "defense," unable to increase staff to grow, and in some cases, unable to increase staff adequately to serve even their existing customer base.

Ultimately, the micro- (firm-level) economics aggregate to the macroeconomic level, where the impact is easier to quantify. We will simply run out of the labor we need to grow. This means that cycles may end sooner or grow significantly slower with consequent risk and volatility. What do we give up? We are a $20 trillion economy growing at a potential rate close to 2 percent a year—that's $400 billion in potential GDP each year. Based on historical precedent, our labor force participation rates, adjusted for age and sex, suggest that our unusual social ills have sapped the labor force of the workers we would need to supply two to three years of additional growth at our baseline pace. Multiply those years of forsaken growth by the value of a year's GDP, and those years' worth of "missing" workers equates to around $1 trillion in forsaken growth. Not someone else's trillion—ours.

An Alternative

It doesn't have to be this way. For the first time in recent memory, the business community is engaging in real problem-solving in US society. Part of this is in response to the millennial workers who demand that their workplaces also have a higher social purpose. The 2016 Cone Communications Millennial Employee Engagement Study found that "64 percent won't take a job if a company doesn't have strong corporate social responsibility (CSR) values."[15] Consumers, and particularly millennial consumers, also expect social responsibility from the companies with which they do business. A 2015 Cone Survey found that 91 percent of this demographic would switch to a brand with a cause.[16]

This effort is happening within the top ranks of American business as well. The prestigious Business Roundtable, whose membership comprises the CEOs of many of the country's largest companies, urged businesses to take a broader view of the purpose of a corporation. Whether adopting that expansive vision or continuing to focus on traditional profit metrics, the demographic landscape is forcing companies to reconsider their talent strategies, and in doing so, focus on the social ills that have befallen our labor force. Adopting successful models of second chance employment not only solves an immediate business need for talent—which must be sustainable and justifiable at that level—it brings the extensive talents of industry into broader challenges. We will focus on measuring the micro and macro benefits of second chance hiring, but the opportunity of employment to impact the lives of employees, their families, and our communities, while not easily quantifiable, is very great indeed.

This begs the question, "Can people with a criminal record be good employees?" Fortunately, in select pockets around the country, across many industries, and largely hidden from public view, business pioneers have already found the answer.

THE PEOPLE
WE CALL "CRIMINAL"

People with criminal records walk around with a
scarlet letter "C" on their foreheads. It doesn't
stand for "Criminal," it stands for "Caught"!
—TOUSSAINT ROMAIN[1]

In the preceding chapter, we offered the bold statement that people with criminal records are the solution to the labor shortage. From a purely quantitative perspective, the numbers are compelling. The sheer quantity of people who have a record suggests that we should question the wisdom of automatically excluding job candidates with records. Quantity, however, does not mean quality. Most employers do not worry about the ability to attract a job applicant, a "quantity" consideration. They are concerned with getting the right candidate— one who can act responsibly and honestly, fit the corporate culture, and stick around. To be a viable workforce solution, people with criminal records have to pass this quality test.

Trial attorney and civil rights activist Toussaint Romain participated in a workforce discussion I led in Charlotte, North Carolina, in April 2019. His memorable exclamation quoted at the outset of this chapter argues that people with criminal records are inherently no different from those without criminal records, and many religious faiths, particularly many Christian beliefs, also argue that all sins have a sort of equality in the sense that they represent failures to adhere to a proper path. Many human services nonprofits, whether faith-based or secular, argue that every person is redeemable.

While I am sympathetic to these bighearted views, the economic model of hiring people with records does not rely on them to be true. Not everyone has to be redeemable. Not everyone has to be employable. To be an effective source of human capital, though, the employer does have to be able to distinguish that subset of the population with records who are indeed ready for employment.

SAME ACT, MULTIPLE OUTCOMES

It goes without saying that operating a motor vehicle after drinking can present a danger to oneself and to others. This act should bear potential consequences, but how it is treated in different jurisdictions and situations underscores the complexities of making assumptions about the existence of a criminal record in a job candidate's background.

Consider a hypothetical situation. Your daughter just finished a tour of duty with the military in the Middle East and came home for a family visit and a party in her honor, where she indulged in an alcoholic beverage. She was stopped by law enforcement on the way home and was asked to take a breathalyzer test. Refusing a breathalyzer is not an option since it results in an automatic suspension of her driving license.

1. If your daughter is twenty years old (underage), she may be subject to zero tolerance policies that could make even a single drink subject to a DUI (driving under the influence) misdemeanor charge (blood alcohol concentration of 0.00–0.02, depending on the state).

2. If she is twenty-one and lives in Utah, a BAC of 0.05 qualifies for a DUI (about two drinks in an hour for a typical woman, compared to three drinks that would typically trigger the 0.08 BAC for a DUI in other states).

3. In many states, a first-time DUI comes with mandatory jail time, typically between twenty-four hours and several days.

4. If a younger sibling or other minor were a passenger in the car, in certain states, this could trigger a felony charge.

5. Or, perhaps, through a judge's leniency or the intervention of an often-costly attorney, the charge was reduced to a traffic violation (e.g., New York State's "Driving While Impaired by Alcohol"), not a DUI misdemeanor.

In all these instances, the same action had different outcomes, including short-term incarceration or a felony record, with all but the last scenario requiring your daughter to "check the Box" if asked about a criminal conviction. None of this excuses the act, but in my experience, these examples have challenged audiences to reexamine their assumptions about the meaning of a criminal conviction.

What the Employer Fears

Let's get it out in the open: there are reasons employers don't jump at the chance to hire people with criminal records. It may have been a bad past experience. It may be well-founded fears or wholly unjustified concerns. Or it may just be a nagging doubt. In my conversations with hundreds of business owners, including those who ultimately started second chance hiring, several key issues came to light, roughly in order: employee safety, public/consumer perception, and employee viability.

Marcus Sheanshang, the CEO of JBM Packaging, a pioneer of second chance employment, of whom the reader will learn more later, stated the safety issue succinctly: "I took this business over from my father, and I hope someday my son and daughter will work here. This has to be a safe place to work for them and every employee." Even if an employer is satisfied that no risk exists, the perceived safety risk can influence others. Existing employees, potential future employees, and customers, past and present, could shun a business that may become known for employees with criminal records.

Customer concerns are not always based on the safety-related fear of contact with ex-offenders. Rob Perez is the founder of DV8 Kitchen, a bakery and café in Lexington, Kentucky, well known for offering second chance employment and largely staffed by recovering addicts. After opening, Rob had difficulty attracting customers. In Rob's words, "People thought second chance meant second rate." It was only after a string of five-star Yelp reviews that customers came— and kept coming for the great food and service. Employers fear that customers will believe that a firm whose staff includes people with records will deliver inferior products and services, a reputation issue.

Beyond the safety concern and reputation risk, businesses worry about the basic ability of people with records to function effectively. At the most basic level, employers want workers who will show up on time, dress appropriately, act responsibly, accept feedback and coaching, work well with others, and do this every working day. The ability to perform in this manner is intrinsically linked to one of character— many employers doubt that people who have transgressed societal norms to the degree that they have a criminal record are capable of this diligence.

Every one of these concerns is valid. They implicitly raise questions about the type of people who have criminal records. Perspective is important. Our workforce argument is not based on a universal statement that every person with a criminal background is redeemable or employable. Just as every job applicant may not be a fit for your company or for a specific open position, not every person with a criminal record needs to be a viable worker. However, for second chance hiring to be a practical staffing strategy, there only need be a significant number of viable candidates from the pool of people who have a criminal record. As we will see in subsequent chapters, not only must this demographic hold a sufficient number of suitable potential employees, but employers need to be able to sort the viable candidates from those who are not.

What Does It Mean to Be a "Criminal"?

It's helpful to have some understanding of what it means to have a criminal record. It is easy to conflate categories and statistics of those who have been touched by the criminal justice system. When an employer utilizes a background check or asks whether a candidate has a criminal record, this broad question incorporates a wide range of historical events, from misdemeanors to felonies to actual incarceration. Further complicating any interpretation is our structure of both state and federal criminal codes. What might be a misdemeanor in one state may be a felony in another. Even within a state, laws may be applied unequally, and the widespread practice of plea bargaining may mean that the crime that generated the actual conviction and record may represent only a piece of the underlying transgression.

The dividing line between the lesser crime of misdemeanors and those of the more serious category of felonies is somewhat arbitrary. As a general rule of thumb, misdemeanors are crimes that can be punished with up to a year in jail, while felonies could involve incarceration within a prison for longer periods. Within that broad category, misdemeanors can be anything from littering to domestic abuse. In other words, a misdemeanor conviction may make someone a "criminal," but, on the surface at least, that categorization reveals very little about the seriousness of the crime or the character of the individual.

Generally, felonies are more serious crimes, but the lines are often blurred. As serious as our perception of felons may be, the reality is more complicated. A felony in one state might be a misdemeanor in another. Felonies can cover very bad behavior or they can refer to obscure statutes that we might not normally associate with criminal behavior. To give one obscure example that was covered in the press at the time, in 2013, a Florida man with his girlfriend released a dozen heart-shaped balloons over a beach and was charged with a third-degree felony under anti-pollution laws.

The data suggest that many felonies are not committed by people whose threat to society should exclude them from employment. One telling statistic from the preceding chapter data (see Figure 9), of nineteen million people with felony convictions, only some seven million experienced incarceration in a prison or formal supervision like post-incarceration parole. *In other words, nearly twelve million of these felons were convicted of crimes that did not even warrant heightened supervision at this level.* In many cases, these twelve million were one-time offenders assigned alternatives to a posttrial prison sentence, whether a short county jail spell (as opposed to prisons, which are used for felony sentences of a year or longer), diversion programs like drug courts, a "suspended sentence" pending successful completion of a period of probation, or "time served," in which pretrial jail time is accepted in lieu of posttrial prison. It is surprising that even earning the label of "convicted felon" may not offer much insight into the crime or the person.

The Demographics of Incarceration

Finally, we come to the ranks of the incarcerated. Surely, anyone with a period of incarceration was guilty of a serious transgression that should concern prospective employers? Even here, in the "Through the Looking Glass" world of the criminal justice system, the answer is not always clear. Misdemeanor charges have at times resulted in long periods of incarceration in jails for those awaiting trial but unable to pay bail. Nearly a half million people in the nation's jails have not been convicted of anything. Even when they are eventually exonerated, the period of incarceration may disrupt their work history and their finances. Those found guilty may be guilty of crimes that did not require incarceration at all, or the sentence associated with the crime might be shorter than the time actually spent incarcerated in advance of a trial. Fortunately, many jurisdictions are changing their policies to avoid pretrial detention, particularly for nonviolent offenses.

The deepest concern, of course, surrounds those who have been declared guilty of a felony and have spent a sentence in prison. Many myths surround the nature of those who have been imprisoned in the United States. It is important to deal with the facts.

The nonprofit Prison Policy Initiative provides excellent insight into the breakdown of the incarcerated population in the United States. A few takeaways from this data:

Someone who was incarcerated may not have ever committed a crime. Among those held in local jails, the majority at any given time have not actually been convicted of anything. In many cases, the pretrial detention of the accused may well be justified as a matter of public safety, but we should also note that the significant number of those are held on "public order" crimes, infractions that could include public drunkenness, personal recreational drug use, prostitution, and so on. In these instances the alleged criminal is unlikely to represent a public safety risk if released pending trial. Detention for these and some of the more serious charges may simply represent a short-term holding period, or could represent a longer-term stay for someone who represents no threat to public safety but does not have the opportunity or ability to post bail.

The prisons are not filled with low-level drug offenders. There is a widespread myth that our prison population is filled with nonviolent, recreational drug users. While it may be true that many other crimes may be connected to substance abuse or the illicit drug trade, the largest cohort among those in prison were convicted of violent crimes, followed by the ranks of those who committed property crimes, with drug crime convictions running a distant third. There is no sugarcoating the nature of the offenses that landed people in prison—these were offenses that did not fall into misdemeanor definitions and generally were serious enough or represented a behavior pattern such that alternatives to incarceration were not applied. There are, of course, some exceptions among any population as large as the US prison population, but the vast majority of people in prison committed crimes that are serious in nature.

I fully accept that sentencing laws are not always appropriate nor evenly applied, and more alternatives to incarceration should be developed, but it is important to recognize that those incarcerated in state and federal prisons committed a serious crime. *It is even more important to realize, however, that a person convicted of a bad action is not necessarily a bad person.*

The Gender and Age Divide

My starting point for gaining a deeper understanding of the criminal as a person starts with the gender divide. One of the striking characteristics of the demographic makeup of the prison system is that it is overwhelmingly male. According to 2015 data from the Bureau of Justice Statistics, 90.6 percent of those in state and federal prisons are men. There is little evidence to suggest that this disparity is because women are extended more leniency than men; female incarceration rates in the United States, while a fraction of the male statistic, are still the highest in the world and have grown at a faster pace over the past few decades. The Prison Policy Initiative also notes a striking difference between the sexes: women are mostly incarcerated in jails, not prisons, suggesting that the commission of serious crimes is more commonly a male endeavor.

The other striking consistency is the relationship between age and crime. This is one of the least controversial areas in criminology and has been recognized for decades. This trend transcends cultural, educational, and economic status differences. Social scientists have found that the tendency to commit a violent criminal act rises in the teen years, peaking around age seventeen, and then declines steadily. The flip side of this statement is to share the oft-stated observation that "people age out of crime."[2]

Age is not an automatic predictor of crime rates, or course, as the variation in the precise relationship over different years suggests other factors are also at work, but we can gain insight into the nature of the people we think of as "criminals" from this data. Putting the transcendent demographic trends together, and the characteristics of those who commit serious crime in particular, we come to the conclusion that the majority of our crime problem is a young male problem. Obviously, the problem of crime in America is much broader than this, but understanding this central tendency is instructive in understanding the nature of many people with a criminal record.

The "Stupid" Male Brain

There are few parents who haven't experienced firsthand the nature of the "teenage brain." Academic papers have generally represented this as a predisposition to "novelty seeking," disproportionately valuing near-term reward over risk, and susceptibility to peer pressure. Parents often assess the risky behavioral outgrowth as "being stupid." Neurological research also points to later development of the male brain, particularly the frontal lobe, which regulates aspects of judgment, and the limbic cortex, which regulates emotion. These are, of course, generalities, and in a US population of three hundred million there will be many exceptions, but our criminal justice system has impacted so many lives that the law of large numbers holds true. These central tendencies have much to tell us about the causes of crime and the nature of criminals. To be more precise, they tell us about the causes of *some* crime and *some* criminals.

This suggests that all too often criminal actions are "crimes of stupidity," committed without full and balanced consideration of the consequences. This by no means excuses the actions, nor does it negate the need for penalties. We should also never lose sight of the fact that many of these actions have inflicted terrible pain and loss on victims.

This sort of recklessness is not attractive to employers. I had a former manager in financial services, one of the top in his field, say to me (I paraphrase): "Stupid employees are the most dangerous. I can build 'fences' around employees with weak moral compasses to limit their behavior, but stupid employees are unpredictable." The statistics that show an "aging out of crime" suggest that this lack of judgment is, on average, not a lifelong condition. Most of us, myself most definitely included, do not want our employers or colleagues to assess our competence today based on our behavior in our teens or early twenties.

It is important to understand that the first act to generate a criminal record may have been an error (and sometimes a horribly serious error) of youth. In a future chapter, we will illustrate the significant barriers to employment, housing, and economic advancement that are generated by even a misdemeanor conviction. It is not hard to see how a youthful "crime of stupidity" can lead to the economic deprivation that leads to "crimes of desperation." This understanding does, however, suggest that many of the errors that led some people to have criminal records are the result of factors that can be outgrown or mediated.

▶ ▶ ▶

How Did We Get Here?

How did we get to such high levels of incarceration and so many Americans with felony and misdemeanor convictions?

Many readers will be familiar with Michelle Alexander's popular book, *The New Jim Crow: Mass Incarceration in the Age of Colorblindness*, which argues that racism was a primary driver of the War on Drugs that saw rising rates of arrest and incarceration. Criticisms of her work, notably by Yale scholar James Forman Jr., author of *Locking Up Our Own: Crime and Punishment in Black America*, argue that her conclusions neglect the reality of rising crime (murder rates in the seventies and eighties were roughly double what they are today), calls at the time from the African American community for more aggressive policing and sentencing, and the reality that drug crimes account for only a small part of the prison population. In her response to these criticisms, Alexander argues that the more aggressive criminal justice approach created a culture of "othering," which persists as a form of racial prejudice.

Whatever one's individual belief on whether racism was the primary driver of the rise, I believe the most constructive lens by which to examine this system is provided by Fordham University scholar John Pfaff. In his book, *Locked In: The True Causes of Mass Incarceration and How to Achieve Real Reform*, Pfaff makes a compelling case that much of the dramatic increase in the number of people with felony convictions was not just a response to a sudden spike in criminal activity nor to increased vigilance in catching serious criminals. Rather, it was a result of decades of prosecutors trained to advance their careers by maximizing the number of felony convictions.

This is closely related to widely acknowledged trends toward "overcriminalization," the trend of adding to the list of actions that represent violations of law. There are further complications and nuances. Alexandra Natapoff, in her excellent book, *Punishment without Crime*, details a runaway misdemeanor system in which *de facto* punishments (fines, fees, jail, loss of job and housing)—coupled with an abusive, but time- and cost-efficient plea bargain system where few crimes are actually investigated and adjudicated—are far more prevalent and punishing than generally understood.

The misdemeanor system, when understood in its full context and consequences, may be unintentionally and unnecessarily driving the pipeline from "crimes of stupidity" to more serious felonies that are "crimes of desperation." Translation: a stupid, relatively minor mistake (a misdemeanor) causes economic consequences that close off other opportunities and drive more serious crimes (felonies).

If this is not depressing enough, we should also underscore the "vicious cycle" that has been created in the United States. The nonprofit organization The Sentencing Project estimated that by 2010 fully one-third of African American men had a felony conviction. This is a stunning number and a driver of intergenerational poverty. Incarcerated fathers and fathers underemployed due to felony records have created communities lacking in role models, where criminal behavior is unduly normalized and where the fundamental "rules of work"—appropriate dress and behavior, negotiating conflicts and obstacles—have never been transmitted to younger generations. Recognizing this impact, which is certainly not exclusive to the African American population, does play a role in structuring models of second chance employment that work for both the employer and the employee.

▶ ▶ ▶

The Critical Question: Are Criminals Bad People?

When we were young, many of us were taught a simplistic version of the criminal justice system: "Policemen arrest bad people," or "Jails are for bad people." There's obviously some truth to these equations—many bad people indeed do things that earn them criminal convictions and even periods of incarceration. But some bad people whom you'd never want to hire—liars and abusive jerks—have no criminal record. And some people who committed crimes have become good people. And some people who committed crimes were not necessarily bad—just some combination of stupid, desperate, victims of trauma, emotionally out of control, intoxicated, and, above all, young.

I pose these questions to the readers, with particular emphasis on their own youthful experiences. Did you ever smoke pot or take any illicit drug? Drive intoxicated? Trespass? Shoplift or otherwise steal? Vandalize? Get into a physical fight? If you answer "yes" to even one of these questions, then you committed a crime. Had you been caught and convicted, you could have rightfully been considered a criminal. Yet the fact that you are reading this book, whose intended audience is primarily current or aspiring business leaders, suggests that you are not a "bad person" or irredeemably unemployable.

Reducing Recidivism: What We Know

My hope is that an employer reading to this point is open to the concept that someone with a criminal record might not be an irredeemable human being. However, if crime is not wholly driven by failures of character, what would prevent someone who had committed a crime from doing it again? An employer's worst nightmare is an act of violence or theft at the workplace. Even crimes committed physically distant from and wholly independent of the workplace carry consequences for the employer: loss of an employee and associated turnover costs as well as the possibility of reputational damage.

It becomes important, then, to understand the conditions that drive "recidivism," the act of someone with a criminal record failing to stay within the bounds of the law and committing another crime. The verb associated with this is to "recidivate." Whether noun or verb, there are some confusing variations in the precise definition and the way this term is applied. Americans often hear of stunningly low recidivism rates in other countries. While there is certainly some truth to better outcomes in other countries, and we certainly can learn practices from others, Oxford scholars Seena Fazel and Achim Wolf in a 2015 study point out that international comparisons are made nearly impossible by disparate definitions of recidivism. In this country, it is common to refer to the widely followed Bureau of Justice Statistics studies of those released from state prisons as recidivism although it technically covers the rates of rearrest. Reconvictions would be lower since not everyone arrested is guilty, nor are those actually guilty always successfully prosecuted. Lower still would be the rates of reincarceration, since even among those found guilty, imprisonment is not always appropriate. The time frame over which recidivism is measured varies widely, although in this country, rates generally refer to either three or five years from release from prisons, or from the date of sentencing when no imprisonment is required. Generally speaking, the US definition is fairly expansive and, on the surface, would make our rates of recidivism look worse in comparison with countries with more narrow definitions. Foreign definitions of recidivism, by comparison, may use time frames as short as six months, and whether a new crime is even counted might depend on the nature of the crime or whether a conviction required imprisonment.

Interestingly, the category of crime committed may tell us little or actually be counterintuitive in assessing the character of felons or their viability as employees. Bureau of Justice Statistics data show that those who commit violent crimes are actually less likely to be rearrested than those who commit property or drug crimes. Taken to its extreme, of those murderers who were eventually released, recidivism is actually dramatically lower than other crimes. In her book, *Life after Murder*, journalist Nancy Mullane chronicles five convicted murderers who were released from prison, but she studied the issue more broadly. In her research, one statistic widely cited has been her tracking of the 988 convicted murderers who had been released from the California state prison system over twenty years. According to her work, none were rearrested for murder, 10 percent for violations of parole, and only 1 percent for a new crime.

National statistics for convicted murders are nowhere near as comforting as Mullane's example, but still suggest rates of rearrest roughly two-thirds of the general average, and consistent with her finding, of those who are rearrested, rarely is it for another murder. Some of this is data bias. At least in theory, the worst of those who committed murders are never released and so are not part of these statistics. Those who are released have generally served a long sentence and are more likely to have "aged out of crime." Those who either serve a sentence shorter than life or have been paroled might have been granted this possibility because the facts surrounding the actual incident or the character of the individual may offer more hope of rehabilitation (e.g., the person who committed a "crime of passion" may be far different than a serial killer). On the flip side, those arrested for property crimes were more likely than average to recidivate. The point is not that employers should be looking to hire ex-murderers, but rather to recognize that the crime of the past does not provide deep insight into the person today.

Essentially, it is not "the what" of the crime that puts someone at a high risk of re-offending, but "the who." The Department of Justice offers some broad characteristics:

> High-risk offenders would have antisocial attitudes, associates, and personalities, or a long criminal history, or substance abuse problems, or poor family relations, and would likely be unemployed. Low-risk offenders, on the other hand, would be fairly prosocial and have good jobs with some, if not many, prosocial contacts. That is, low-risk offenders likely have good jobs, good relationships with their families, good relationships with prosocial acquaintances, fairly prosocial attitudes, a limited criminal history, and few if any substance abuse problems.[3]

Of course, many of the traits associated with high risk of re-offending can be treated through a variety of programs within the correctional system. Diversion programs—alternatives to incarceration that provide a combination of social services and supervision—are generally shown to be effective at reducing recidivism, particularly for the first-time and lower-level offenders they typically serve. One program that particularly impressed me is the MENTOR Court system in Philadelphia, the brainchild of Judge Michael Erdos. Like other diversion programs in lieu of incarceration, treatment programs are administered through court-employed social workers while the court judge delivers accountability and supervision. MENTOR adds another layer—each of the participants in the program is assigned a volunteer community mentor with a structured communication plan; many of the mentors are themselves people who have rebuilt their lives following convictions and incarceration.

When I began my studies of people with criminal records as a potential workforce, I quickly learned that employment is a "necessary but not sufficient" condition. Even low-paying employment reduces recidivism by more than 20 percent, so a paycheck is critical but does not address the whole spectrum of forces that drive re-offending.

Most of the studies directly relating to recidivism focus on in-prison programming to reduce recidivism. Broadly, these can be categorized in two ways: changing hearts and changing minds. Paths focusing on changing hearts address many of the characteristics of high-risk re-offenders cited above: antisocial attitudes and personalities, substance abuse, and poor family relations. In technical terms, this would include cognitive behavioral programs that promote self-reflection on the part of participants to understand and change the patterns of thinking and emotion that have led not only to illegal choices, but also have led to broken relationships. Perhaps unsurprisingly, "changing hearts" seems to be the more critical factor.

Among the most established routes to changing hearts has been the strong tradition of prison ministry in the United States. These have long preceded more recent secular initiatives intended to reduce recidivism. The Prison Fellowship, an organization founded by convicted Watergate conspirator Charles Coulson, is among the better known and widely established programs, but many such ministries exist even at the most local level. I have met many returning citizens whose lives were truly changed by prison ministry.

Secular rehabilitation programs have also proven very beneficial in changing hearts. Reaching Out from Within is one such program that operates in prisons in Kansas and North Carolina. Its curriculum centers around a four-hundred-page "Blue Book," which offers a weekly guide stressing nonviolence and personal development that has been tested through thirty years of experience. The documentary *Big Sonia* memorialized one of the sessions where inmates' lives are impacted in a dialogue with a ninety-year-old Holocaust and concentration camp survivor, Sonia Warshawski. The program has a strong track record of reducing recidivism.

If programs to change hearts impact the antisocial attitudes that drive re-offending, programs to change minds seek more concrete training that can help with providing employment. The RAND Corporation, a think tank, found that pure education, as opposed to vocational training, was the most effective at reducing recidivism. This may reflect the very low levels of educational attainment found within the prison population, so education is simply providing basic literacy and numeracy skills that are fundamental to job growth. I have also heard criticisms that too many in-prison vocational programs are not responsive to future job needs, and suffer in comparison, although I believe this is changing.

Education beyond the basics may also be beneficial because it helps participants overcome the many credentialing requirements that are part of a modern job search. Beyond a high school diploma or GED (General Education Development tests, considered equivalent to a high school diploma), in-prison college degree programs impart deeper knowledge, further broaden the opportunities to simply be considered for a job, signify a level of dedication to rehabilitation to potential employers, and offer a post-release network and community. The Bard Prison Initiative, founded in 1999, has been granting associate degrees since 2005 and bachelor's degrees since 2008. It is the focus of the four-part PBS documentary *College behind Bars,* of which Ken Burns is the executive producer. It currently enrolls approximately three hundred students, has six hundred graduates, and has led a national consortium of fifteen colleges and universities to broaden educational opportunities nationally. We should keep in mind that there is a data bias in looking at college programs and recidivism—those who successfully complete these programs are already among the cognitive elite of the prison population and have a demonstrated desire to improve themselves, so such a demographic could already be expected to have lower recidivism. Nonetheless, the results of the Bard program are impressive: 97.5 percent of its graduates have not returned to prison.

Outside the Prison Environment

One aspect of recidivism that has (deservedly) gained the attention of criminal justice reform advocates is the issue of "technical violations" as a cause for rearrest and reimprisonment. Probation and parole generally are conditional forms of freedom—failure to adhere to the terms ("violation") of this supervision often leads to reincarceration. In theory, this makes sense, protecting the public from unrehabilitated former prisoners. In practice, however, technical violations that result in reincarceration can lead to disproportionate punishment that disrupts actual rehabilitation.

A TALE OF TWO TECHNICAL VIOLATIONS

I am a strong believer in the maxim that "the plural of anecdote is not data." It is important not to extrapolate single examples into an overarching belief. In the world of criminal justice, however, consistency of anecdotes—hearing the same story over and over again, particularly across different parts of the country—has led me to ask better questions or gain greater insight into actual data.

A business owner in Indianapolis, a multistate contractor in the commercial construction industry, shared the story of a second chance hire who was a diligent employee. The man had been paroled from prison (i.e., early release, subject to conditions). Their work took them to Georgia and ended up requiring an unexpectedly longer time out of state. This worker, eager to please his employer, did not object nor did he have the life skills to communicate that this would make him miss meetings with his parole officer, a technical violation. Upon their return, the worker was reincarcerated for this violation.

In northern Ohio, another business owner related a parallel story. He hired a man who had been paroled from prison and who became an excellent employee. Uncharacteristically, he did not show for work one day and did not answer calls to his cell phone. Unbeknownst to the employer, the worker had numerous traffic violations that had gone unpaid when he entered prison decades earlier. These penalties compounded to a balance of several hundred dollars, but this newly returned citizen was not yet able to pay them off while he rebuilt his life and finances. His driver's license, which he needed to commute to work, had been suspended. This employee was caught driving with a suspended license, a technical parole violation, and was returned to prison to serve several remaining years of his sentence.

Scholars like John Pfaff argue that many technical violations are actually reflections of the commission of a much more serious crime, or "pretextual violations." From a prosecutor's standpoint, it is far faster and easier to incarcerate someone on the basis of a parole violation than to build a case for a new prosecution. This suggests that those reincarcerated for technical violations were generally deserving of imprisonment.

Even if one accepts Pfaff's proposition as the rule, anecdotal evidence abounds (see sidebar) that there are a significant number of exceptions. A 2017 nationwide survey by The Marshall Project estimates that more than 61,000 of the total of those incarcerated (about 2.3 million) were there for technical violations, and this is likely an undercount.[4] In percentage terms, this may be small, but we should never lose sight that these exceptions reflect the freedom and lives of real individuals. When these exceptions occur, we are unjustly depriving people of freedom, impairing their ability to rebuild their lives, and yes, denying employers and the economy of a resource. We also learn once again, that, in the American justice system, generalities are dangerous and the fact of a record and incarceration must be examined on an individual basis.

In one sense, none of this is directly relevant to our models of employment. As citizens, we should care about broader issues of justice, but as employers, we have more narrow concerns. We are fortunate to have data that addresses those issues.

The Evidence: Studies Large and Small

Ultimately, from an economic standpoint, the question is not truly "Are these good people?" We will never know what is in an employee's heart. We can only ask whether, as employees, they can behave in ways that employers associate with good character: Do they work honestly and diligently? Can people with criminal records be good employees?

Ultimately, opinion does not matter, but data does. There is admittedly a limited amount of formal data. But there are a number of organizations that have deliberately focused on identifying people with criminal records for employment, developing systems that select and support success, and tracking the result.

The issue of why data is so scarce is both interesting and frustrating. On a practical level, I have found that many larger employers simply don't track the performance of hires with a criminal record— once someone is an employee, it simply does not occur to them to monitor any group of employees based on any background criterion, whether criminal record, schooling, or any other background characteristic. Sometimes, particularly among employers who are consciously driving second chance hiring, this is for moral reasons. These employers don't believe second chance hires should ever be perceived as different from any other employee. Finally, people in criminal justice reform have shared with me their belief that there are some companies tracking these statistics, but do not want to make this public because of the perceived reputational risk to their business. While I can respect such sentiments, it leads to a paucity of data that, were it more plentiful, would be helpful in driving other companies to adopt more inclusive hiring standards.

Given these barriers to data collection, we are fortunate to have The Johns Hopkins Health System. More than fifteen years ago, Johns Hopkins began selectively hiring people with criminal records. As the size of this cohort grew and progressed, Johns Hopkins assessed the performance of these hires. After completing a five-year study with nearly five hundred hires with criminal records, the hospital was able to draw favorable conclusions. In comparison with traditional hires, those with criminal records experienced lower turnover in the first forty months. The hospital paid special attention to those hires who had a record for a violent crime; of those seventy-nine who were tracked for a period of three to six years, seventy-three were still employed by Johns Hopkins, and only one had been involuntarily terminated.

It is fair for an employer to wonder whether, of those hires with criminal records who did not remain employed, were there any exceptional problems. The hospital made one other important observation to address this concern. Like any other employer, Johns Hopkins had a number of terminations that it characterized as "problematic"—but none of there were ex-offenders.

Johns Hopkins's commitment to second chance employment offers one additional lesson. In the *US News & World Report*'s 2019–2020 list, Johns Hopkins is ranked the number three adult hospital in the nation among the 4,600 included in the study. This was the thirtieth consecutive year that the institution was among the top hospitals in the United States. Second chance does not mean second rate.

Another large organization, the US military, has offered a unique insight into the job performance of people with criminal records. The military is often considered the largest employer in country with more than 2.1 million serving on active duty, reserve, and in the National Guard in 2018. The military has traditionally barred applicants with felony convictions (including state-level misdemeanors that would qualify as felonies under the Uniform Code of Military Justice). However, under continuing challenge from the demands of the Global War on Terror, and with increasing competition from private sector employers, the Department of Defense has expanded the use of its felony waiver program. These waivers, which are granted selectively, offer people with records the opportunity to enter the military, serve their country, and develop a career that would otherwise be unavailable.

The US military itself has published no study of the results of the waiver program. However, using Freedom of Information Act requests, sociologists Jennifer Hickes Lundquist, Devah Pager, and Eiko Strader gathered the relevant data. The scholars tracked the performance of 1.3 million enlistees (those with and without felony records) from 2002 to 2009. There is a likely skew to some of the results since those with felony records are more likely to be assigned to roles with higher risk and associated stress (e.g., combat). This shows, for instance, that enlistees with serious criminal records have a higher rate of death. Perhaps also related to the specific nature of the military assignment, enlistees with a criminal record are slightly more likely to be discharged for a criminal offense than those with no history, 6.6 percent vs. 5 percent.[5]

The critical findings, however, are very encouraging, not just for the military felony waiver program but also by implication for any employer considering second chance employment. Short-term turnover in the military is already very limited, but enlistees with a record have no higher attrition than those without. In performance, though, as measured by promotion to the rank of sergeant or higher, enlistees with a felony conviction excelled:

> To the extent that those with felony waivers differ from those without, it is in the direction of more successful advancement through the ranks. Despite widespread concerns about the competence of individuals with serious criminal histories, these analyses suggest that ex-felons screened into military service meet and exceed standards of performance.[6]

When examining promotions after six years of service, those with a felony conviction were more than 32 percent more likely to achieve the rank of sergeant or higher. Pay grade increases for those with felony records were also clearly faster than for other enlistees.

The American Civil Liberties Union (ACLU) has also collected a number of single-employer studies. The most notable characteristics in these studies are the low turnover rates associated with second chance hiring. The experience of Total Wine & More, a liquor retail chain with seven-thousand-plus employees, is among the examples cited in the ACLU publication *Back to Business: How Hiring Formerly Incarcerated Job Seekers Benefits Your Company*. On average, first-year turnover rates for hires with criminal records was more than twelve full percentage points lower than traditional hires. In another example, Electronic Recyclers International reduced its turnover rate by more than half through a program recruiting people with criminal records.[7]

These examples also align with my own research and experience with second chance employers. In one of the most notable examples, Dan Meyer, CEO of Nehemiah Manufacturing, estimates that by largely staffing through second chance hires, he has increased his business's cash flow (EBITDA) by 5.2 percent. In his consumer products manufacturing business, 130 of his 180 employees are second chance hires (a broad interpretation includes people with records, battling addiction, and who are homeless). His estimate of the financial benefit of low turnover takes into account the loss of hours worked, recruiting expenses, and lost productivity. A team from Harvard Business School visited Nehemiah to write a case study, the first business school case specifically studying a second chance employer.

A Practical Bottom Line

Ultimately, we don't know what exact percentage of people with a criminal record can be viable employees, but we can say with certainty that this demographic pool is large enough and underutilized enough to be an enormous business opportunity. Even if we take the historically hardest to employ, those with a recent history of incarceration, I estimate that roughly a third walk out of the prison gates ready for employment, another third can be made ready, and the final third, whether for reasons of mental illness, incurable addiction, or moral character, are not viable employees. But that's more than enough given the vast size of this labor pool.

Our model is not about creating a path to employment for everyone. Our model is employer-centric, finding the people who can fill a business's need for labor. This does not mean that this model will not do social good. Even if our strategies ultimately mean that employers are hiring the "cream of the crop" among those with records, that will free more resources for those who are not yet ready (or may never be ready) for employment. Certainly, for those we can employ, the benefits of employment are meaningful: the potential for financial security and breaking cycles of multigenerational poverty, improved public safety, and the well-being of families and communities.

The fact that there are large numbers of people with criminal records, many of whom can be viable employees, is in itself insufficient to support a talent acquisition model. Businesses need a model of success, and that model has to be replicable, scalable, and profitable. We will explore the model that works—and those that fail—in Chapter Four.

In this chapter, we have largely defined people with records numerically and in aggregate. In the next chapter, we'll approach the issue of criminal record and character from a different perspective. As individuals, we are shaped by our experiences, and the journey from incarceration to rehabilitation, "reentry," has much to say about returning citizens as employees.

Turn the page!

REENTRY

*If employers truly understood what it takes to
rebuild your life, they'd view it as a badge.*
—BO FROWINE, *Executive Director
of the Charlotte Mecklenburg Dream Center*[1]

What do we truly know about the character of a job applicant with a criminal record? The statistics of the preceding chapter inform us about the people convicted of crimes as a group. The criminal record itself perhaps gives us a snapshot of that person at the moment the act was committed. But what do we know of the person today? More than you would think. The journey of the job applicant with a criminal record, particularly one whose path started as he or she exited prison, can inform the employer about the job-seeker's character.

In December 2016, along with a researcher from Georgetown University, I presented at an "Open Impact" session at the University of Chicago's Polsky Center for Entrepreneurship and Innovation on the topic of second chance hiring. Open to a broader community, the interactive program on second chance employment was advertised within the graduate schools of that great university. Students from the Law School participated. Students from the School of Social Service Administration participated. A student from the Pritzker School of Medicine was there as was an interested member of the general public. It is interesting that not a single student from the highly regarded Booth School of Business attended.

I may have been the "expert," but the audience did the most important teaching that day. These sessions were intended to be interactive, under the expert guidance of the senior associate director of the Polsky Center, Will Gossin, who acted as facilitator. In the evening's most memorable activity, Will rolled out a large whiteboard and drew a horizontal line nearly the entire width of the board. He identified this construct as a timeline. Just to the left of the line, Will drew a stick figure standing outside a building with barred windows—identifying the start of the timeline as the moment of release from incarceration. On the right of the line was that same figure standing outside a building with belching smokestacks, a factory with employment opportunities. In other words, the timeline represented the journey from leaving prison to job application.

Each table in the room had pens and yellow sticky note pads. Will challenged each table to write down a single task that the returning citizen had to accomplish on his journey from incarceration to job application and place that task at an appropriate spot on the timeline. After a buzz of discussion, the session participants rose from the tables and started to place the yellow squares on the whiteboard. Many tasks sparked a discussion resulting in additional tasks: "You need to submit an application online." "Well, then you need access to a computer." "I suppose you need to learn how to use a computer." "You need a résumé." Within minutes, the center of the timeline was filled with a mountain of tasks.

By the end of the exercise, it became apparent that the job applicant, recently released from prison, who may have had no recent work experience and no advanced education, was indeed a person of great accomplishment. This person was a successful "mountain climber," overcoming obstacle after obstacle just to be in a position to apply for an entry-level job. Employers could not ask for a better test of character than the willingness to face fear, humiliation, ostracization, and invest copious amounts of time and energy, all to try to do the right thing with an uncertain return and a best-case scenario of a lower-wage job. Yet this is common for people coming out of prison.

"Reentry simulations" are structured exercises that allow participants an opportunity to glimpse the challenges faced by second chance job applicants. Many of us learned, "Don't judge a man until you've walked a mile in his shoes," and while a reentry simulation may not be even a full mile stroll, it is a good starting point for understanding the character of second chance applicants.

Reentry simulations were inspired by another worthwhile project, poverty simulations. Originally created in the 1970s, these simulations have been updated by the nonprofit Missouri Community Action Network, which licenses simulation kits as "Community Action Poverty Simulation (CAPS)" and provides training to facilitators. Participants in CAPS are assigned an identity of one of twenty-six families facing poverty, based on actual stories of people served by the Missouri nonprofit. Over the course of the two- to four-hour simulation, participants role-play a month in the life of their characters, navigating bureaucracies, health challenges, transportation, and food and housing security. The CAPS kits are used by more than two thousand organizations worldwide, but increasingly have been

adopted by chambers of commerce and even companies as tools
to educate future business leaders. Such organizations understand
that our economy benefits from the participation of all potential
workers, and employers who understand the needs and challenges
of low-income families are better able to tap the potential of this
demographic.

Reentry simulations are parallel exercises designed to highlight
the numerous challenges faced by people leaving incarceration.
Jeff Abramowitz is the executive director of reentry services for
Philadelphia-based JEVS Human Services, one of the largest social
service organizations in Pennsylvania, and is a nationally recognized
expert on the challenges of reentry. He has designed and leads reentry
simulations around the country. Abramowitz also has experienced
five years in federal prison.

As a friend, he wanted to attend a talk I was giving at the Philadelphia Federal Reserve Bank. Because of his record, we did not know
whether he would even be permitted through security (he was). As
we walked to the Federal Reserve together, he pointed out the building where he had been held after his guilty verdict, pending transfer
to prison. He recounted his memory of sitting naked in the cell,
while guards argued over who would get to keep his suit.

Abramowitz led me through parts of his own path home and the
journeys he has witnessed in his role with JEVS. He shared some important context:

> The most challenging part of my time was when I came home. Most
> people can navigate life in prison—everything is taken care of, food,
> housing, where you are going to be. There's also an expectation that
> when you come home, there's this freedom. There isn't—I was more
> restricted in the halfway house than in prison.

The starting point for that journey was when he left the prison gates in western Pennsylvania en route to the transitional facility in Philadelphia. He was given a four-hour time limit to register at the halfway house or risk being in violation of his release terms, something that could have sent him right back to prison. His daughter picked him up and drove him back. Because they stopped for a sandwich, he almost missed the check-in. Those without a ride are given a bus ticket and the challenge of navigating transportation to their destination beyond the bus station. Tasks we take for granted—the ability to use a cell phone to access the internet for directions and schedules, for instance—all are unlikely to be accessible on that challenge.

Abramowitz spent his half decade in prison teaching and helping other inmates prepare for post-release success. When he left the gates of the facility, he was given a preloaded debit card with $22.48. His daughter brought him toiletries and bed linens, most of which were confiscated on his entry to the halfway house. Other residents contributed part of their supplies to the newcomer, a common ritual at that facility. His brother supplemented that with $100 so he could purchase some clothing and an old flip phone.

Most prison systems give exiting inmates some money that is intended, at least in theory, to be a stake to get them started toward rehabilitation. Some systems will provide a bus ticket as well, while others expect that returning citizens must take transportation expenses out of the "gate money" they provide. The Marshall Project, the nonprofit criminal justice journalism organization, surveyed states to find how much gate money each state prison system provided. Of the forty-two states that responded, California was the most generous with $200, Colorado next with $100, and then it quickly dropped to typical payments of far lower amounts. In some cases, the amount of gate money had been set in the 1970s and never adjusted for decades of inflation.[2] It is true that some states make case-by-case allowances, or have given inmates the chance to earn meager amounts of money in prison, but even the most diligent worker and saver is unlikely to have enough to go far.

Money is just one part of the complex puzzle that must be solved before a returning citizen can have any hope of employment. Abramowitz, with a college education, a graduate degree, and years of experience as an attorney, was better equipped than most who leave prison. He still admits, "The navigation to employment is the hardest part." For people who have spent decades in prison, the transition to an online economy and smartphones may simply have passed them by. Even those who have been incarcerated for shorter periods have been in such a structured environment that returning to face the complexities of everyday life can be overwhelming, let alone when the collateral consequences of a criminal record are added to the mix. In the reentry simulations that Abramowitz runs, he provides a partial list of the interactions, obstacles, obligations, and resources that many returning citizens must successfully navigate: Department of Motor Vehicles, probation/parole officer meetings, court obligations, completing a GED, opening a bank account, finding and keeping employment, applying for social services, pawnshop loans, landlords/rent, transportation, housing, and services for physical and mental health.

Even before tackling most of these interactions, a foundational step is gathering the documentation needed to function in the modern world. Many people who become involved in the justice system either did not have stable housing and family before prison or lost it during their incarceration. Social Security cards, birth certificates, training and education certifications (possibly earned before digitization of records), all may be lost. For many returning citizens, regaining a driver's license is one of the first hurdles—licenses aren't typically revoked unless relevant to the conviction, but often have expired or been suspended due to unpaid fines. A comment on the Jobs for Felons Hub website, a compendium of helpful information for people with records, illustrates the sort of challenges the simplest tasks can represent:

> I'm researching for my brother who will be released in a few months. Getting a new license will not be easy. He will have to show "proof of residency" along with his birth certificate and Social Security (he has both of these). How do you show proof of residency? He'll be living with someone, doesn't pay any utilities, doesn't have an apartment because he won't have any ID. It seems like a catch-22 situation.

Even for those who eventually hold a license, the cost of a car may be prohibitive. Public transit access may be limited and is its own expense. For those who either were not required to go to a halfway house or who have left that kind of facility, affordable housing is a tremendous challenge, and some may resort to "couch surfing" among friends and relatives, with the lack of a permanent address further complicating restoring identification and applying for social services and work. While juggling all this, many are working to complete a GED to improve their job prospects through training.

There have been improvements in the reentry planning and support in prisons, but they have not been universally adopted. Correctional authorities are increasingly focused on better outcomes for justice-involved individuals. Abramowitz acknowledged some of the challenges: "Successful reentry back into society is something which is difficult. It is a complex process and unpredictable process . . . each person has different individual needs, resources, and histories."

Nonprofits often fill in the missing pieces. Abramowitz's JEVS provides returning citizens with a broad array of support through transit passes, clothing, résumé writing, education classes, and numerous social services, but resources are not unlimited. He developed some of his programming while in prison; he found that the federal facility where he was incarcerated lacked reentry planning, so as an inmate he developed and taught his own program, "Get Ready. Get Set. Get Out." Public/private partnerships are also growing. The Securus Foundation partnered with the Cuyahoga County (Cleveland region) Office of Reentry to introduce their reentry planning tool, the Exodus Planner, hoping to create an effective model that can be replicated elsewhere.[3]

Other business leaders have been applying their technological prowess to create solutions through nonprofits they have founded. Ray Dalton's relink.org charity deployed a mobile site directory of resources (relink.org), searchable by geography and service required. Patricia Egipciaco, an IT professional passionate about expanding opportunities for justice-involved individuals, founded the nonprofit My Rebuilt Life. Its website (www.myrebuiltlife.org) provides a cloud-based portal to manage career credentials, access stored life documents, and access thousands of free college courses. Of course, web-based and mobile-based support also requires ready access to the internet. In a world where so many applications and services are processed online, some returning citizens must first conquer basic computer literacy and find access to a computer.

Even if a returning citizen is able to secure employment with the support of all these resources, the challenges do not end. Money issues may start with "gate money," but they can persist for years. Paychecks to returning citizens may simply not go as far as for the general population. Many people with felonies, particularly those who have recently exited incarceration, are unbanked. Paychecks are reduced by check-cashing fees, and borrowing is facilitated by pawnshops, with accompanying fees driving effective interest rates well into the double and even triple digits. From the remaining pay, some will also have to pay restitution costs to victims of their crime. Many will also pay "supervision fees" that go, at least in theory, to reimbursing the taxpayer for some of the cost of a parole officer. Others may be required to pay the costs of addiction treatment programs or other services that may be required as a condition of parole.

No matter how well planned the reentry, any outcome that does not include employment and economic opportunity will likely not succeed. And for that to happen, we must learn to recognize achievement and character even when they come in different forms.

Many decades ago, I was responsible for hiring and managing entry-level sales positions in financial services. These positions had upside career potential with seven-figure incomes, and also had incredibly high failure rates. The best predictor of success was a track record of existing accomplishment. My single most important interview question was, "Can you describe to me a major challenge you have faced—it may have been personal, professional, or while in school—and how you worked to overcome it?"

Once, I was interviewing candidates for a single position, and it came down to two final applicants. The first was a man in his late thirties with a résumé that showed a steady progression in his career. When I posed the question to him, he looked thoughtful, and after a long pause, shook his head and responded, "I don't really have any examples—I guess I've just been lucky." The second was a woman of similar age, who had come from a conservative Iranian immigrant family. Her husband had divorced her, a mark of shame in her culture. She described to me how, for the first time in her life, after more than a decade as an adult without independence and sequestered from the broader world, she had to open her own bank account, land her first job, and find her first apartment. I offered her the position.

The journey of reentry, fully understood, can be a testament to character, deserving of recognition by employers.

SUCCESS IS
NOT RANDOM

*Would you rather pay someone $30,000 to do
a job, or pay $30,000 to keep someone in jail?*
— DAN MEYER, CEO and Founder,
Nehemiah Manufacturing[1]

Dan Meyer posed this question to me when I first met him in 2016, as I was visiting his Cincinnati factory. While Dan meant this rhetorically, it is actually a serious question. The answer for Dan is the first choice: pay someone to work, because hiring people who might otherwise recidivate or become incarcerated has the potential to result in superior business performance.

Dan's success was no accident. While he was one of the first (and one of the best) second chance employers I would meet, it soon became apparent that he was not alone. There is no directory of companies that consciously pursue second chance employment, and virtually no scholarly literature that has studied these businesses. However, through internet searches, networking, and eventually building a reputation as a researcher interested in these businesses, I have had the good fortune to meet many companies that have successfully pursued second chance hiring.

Why did these employers choose to pursue people in need of a second chance? The most common answer was religious conviction, particularly evangelical Christianity. A few employers became interested because of personal experience with the criminal justice system, having either been arrested themselves or witnessed the experience of a close friend or family member. Occasionally, an executive stumbled into this through a single exceptionally successful hire and realized that this success could be replicated. Some were motivated by other principles or life experience. Increasingly, the visible success of second chance employers is a key catalyst for other companies to adopt second chance hiring.

From a purely business perspective, motivation didn't matter. Geography didn't matter. Even industry didn't matter. What counted was the processes that each company deployed to make this employee staffing model work. To my amazement, when successful second chance employers in different parts of the country and different lines of business shared their systems with me, I recognized that each had come to the same set of processes. In other words, there is a right way to do this, a model of success.

With so many convictions in the United States, employees with criminal records are all around us. We never really know the background of the call center employee with whom we just spoke, the restaurant workers who prepared our meal or served us, our neighbors, colleagues, the person who built our car or painted our home.

Many people who've made mistakes in their past have successfully rebuilt their lives. From the perspective of filling our labor shortage, most of these people will not be readily accessible candidates for hiring; they are already on their own career paths and many are no more available than any other already-employed worker in the economy. There are still some opportunities to lift this population to higher levels of employment from which their records may have barred them. Ultimately, however, the solution to our labor shortage lies with those who are truly marginalized from the labor market: out of the workforce, unemployed, or underemployed at levels of compensation and contribution well below their potential.

The Wrong Way and the Right Way

It is important to remember that no model of hiring is perfect. Companies that do not consider candidates with criminal records do not have 100 percent perfect employees. For companies with hundreds or thousands of employees, the statistical "law of large numbers" tends to produce a bell-curve-shaped distribution. Companies with strong management cultures seek to remove weak performers and foster the development of their workers. Competitive compensation, whether in cash, benefits, or flexibility, tends to lift the average quality of the hiring pool and retain strong contributors. Those companies shift the curve "to the right," toward a higher-quality average, but the variances remain. So, too, not every experience with a second chance hire is a "win" for the employer. Just as companies without second chance hiring can "shift the curve" and impact the quality of their workforce, companies that do consider candidates with criminal records develop processes that can shape the quality of their hires.

VISUALIZING THE MODELS OF SECOND CHANCE HIRING

Like many people in business, I rely heavily on graphs as easy ways to visualize complex data. The charts below reflect not hard data but are derived from conversations with hundreds of businesspeople over the years. They offer a way to conceptualize different modes of second chance employment, showing how the addition of second chance employees compares in quality to a traditional workforce.

TRADITIONAL CANDIDATE ONLY

Companies that employ only traditional candidates have an average level of employee quality and a distribution of better and worse performers.

Companies that add second chance hires but are driven by the primary goal of cheap labor are neither highly selective nor do they invest in retention and development of employees. Second chance hires in this model generally perform worse than traditional hires.

DISPOSABLE EMPLOYEE MODEL

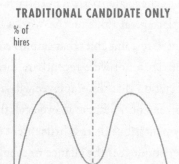

TRADITIONAL CANDIDATE ONLY

% of
hires

worse   < Quality of Hires >   better

The most common experience is businesses that are selective in their hiring but make no accommodation for the special needs often associated with people with criminal records. They follow the Undifferentiated Model. Those employees who succeed display the typical attributes of successful second chance hires: grit, determination, and loyalty. But without support, poor outcomes are just as likely: hires who have poor attendance, struggle with relationships with coworkers or supervisors, or relapse into substance abuse.

The final model, the True Second Chance Model, shows the full potential of hiring people with criminal records. Sourced and supported right, these are hires who more than repay the investment in adopting this model. They offer employers high engagement, low turnover, and strong productivity.

TRUE SECOND CHANCE MODEL

% of
hires

worse   < Quality of Hires >   better

Many employers have had some experience in hiring people with criminal records. Although actual data on this second chance hiring is limited or simply nonexistent, the accompanying charts conceptually illustrate the outcomes experienced by companies with different approaches. There are, essentially, three models of hiring people with criminal records, only one of which concerns us.

The first is the Disposable Employee Model, where people with criminal backgrounds are hired as cheap alternatives in entry-level jobs. In this model, employers place great value on the Work Opportunity Tax Credit that is granted to companies that employ candidates with a recent felony conviction or were recently released from prison. There is little expectation that the employee will stay long, let alone have career advancement. I hesitate to even call this a form of second chance employment, since there is little intent on the part of the employer to offer employees the chance to rebuild their lives. Relative to a normal distribution curve of worker quality, this model will skew toward weaker employees. This is not always a matter of character—these employees are not empowered to contribute at a higher level. Given the demographic argument for long-term labor force challenges set forth in the Introduction, this model is neither of interest to me, nor do I think it is a viable staffing strategy over the long run. In the labor-scarce future, employers cannot afford to treat their workers as if there is a never-ending stream of replacements.

The second model of hiring people with criminal records is the most common, which for sake of clarity, we can categorize as the Undifferentiated Model. This is found among employers with a genuine long-term interest in their workforce and who value the current welfare and career advancement of employees. Among these employers who embrace a holistic approach are those who currently or in the past have given consideration to applicants with a criminal record, but have not done so with a conscious, planned effort. Their sourcing and support for people with criminal records are undifferentiated from traditional hiring practices. While there is no formal evaluation of their success, anecdotally there is a consistent picture. Among other concerns, employers of this kind report fairly high turnover for the second chance demographic, typically at levels similar to sourcing models like staffing agencies.

There is another consistent theme in this Undifferentiated Model: senior executives and owners of these companies have found that the quality of people with criminal records is not distributed along the bell curve of their traditional hires; the clustering around an average does not occur. Rather, there is a "barbell" with employees clustering either around worse-than-average or better-than-average characteristics relative to traditional hires. Anecdotally, many employers using the Undifferentiated Model have shared with me that hires with criminal records were either the best employees or the worst employees. On the face of it, this Undifferentiated Model might still suggest a reasonable approach. After all, the average of "best" and "worst" is, well, "average." The reality for employers, however, is that the damage, cost, time, and effort associated with a single bad employee more than outweighs the benefits of a good employee. Many employers who have participated in such Undifferentiated Models no longer offer second chance employment.

All these models seem to contradict the good results experienced by Johns Hopkins and others as outlined in Chapter Two. To put it bluntly, there's a right way and a wrong way to hire people with criminal records. As a business proposition, the Disposable Employee Model is dead wrong, and the Undifferentiated Model is insufficient. There is another way—a model that is not a theoretical construct but one created by business owners and senior executives, refined through trial, error, and business acumen and vision. It is a model that has worked across industries and geographies.

It is the one that works.

The True Second Chance Model is the distillation of the wisdom and experience of businesses that have succeeded in creating hiring processes for people with criminal records, as well as those marginalized by homelessness, addiction, and other social ills. The result of this model is that, relative to the overall workforce, the quality of these second chance hires "skews right"—in other words, this model creates a disproportionate number of above-average workers. It is not foolproof—there are still employees who are worse than average, but employers who have embraced this model reap the benefits outlined in Chapter Two: low turnover and high engagement, with resulting cost savings and productivity improvement (see Figure 10).

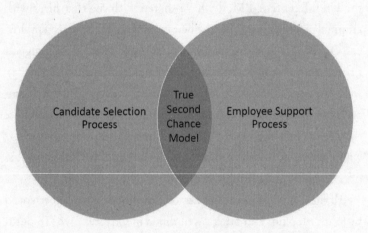

Figure 10: The Building Blocks of Success

The Key: Process and Partners

Conceptually, the True Second Chance Model of employment could not be simpler. To achieve the benefits of sourcing loyal and engaged employees from the ranks of those with criminal records, companies need to develop and implement two sets of processes. The first system identifies who among the job-seekers are ready for employment, and the second system supports their continued employment. The reality of actually implementing and refining these processes requires extensive time, patience, and focus of pioneering business leaders. We are fortunate that we can learn from their mistakes and experience. Like any other investment in your business, implementing the True Second Chance Model is not a "free lunch," but emulating the best practices of these business leaders can help ensure that your business can maximize the returns in terms of quality employees, dedicated to their work and loyal to their employer.

The first system, a candidate-selection process—that is, determining who is ready for employment—sounds no different than any standard interview process. For the candidate who, despite a criminal record, has a well-established and solid employment history, there is no need for a different initial screening. Even in these cases, employers still need to establish whether the candidate's background can cause reputational risk, regulatory problems, or is consistent with other company values. The primary "readiness" screen is a character screen. As outlined earlier, the category of criminal offense, when measured strictly by recidivism rates, offers limited insight into the character of the person and can even be counterintuitive. Even the most robust single indicator, the age of the individual ("aging out of crime"), is still, on its own, an inadequate screen. While reviewing such factors plays a role later in the review process, assessment of job readiness is an assessment of character, and holistically sizing up the character of an applicant requires a great deal of time. The successful second chance employers know there are others who can and do have the ability to do this holistic assessment. More on this later.

A critical component of successful second chance hiring is the willingness to accept candidates who have the "grit" and "heart" to rebuild their lives, but have had extremely limited experience and mentorship. In dealing with traditional candidate populations, finding a person of character who can do the job generally suffices. However, many people in need of a second chance, particularly those coming from incarceration or otherwise exiled from work, may be people of character, but they need more. It is not enough that they are ready and willing to work; they may need additional tools and accommodations to maintain employment.

When employers hear the word *accommodation*, they are often concerned about cost and effort. Context is important. Employers are already making accommodations on a regular basis, everything from the Ping-Pong table in the break room for the millennials to flex hours to job sharing to parental leave policies to employee assistance programs (EAP)—all are accommodations to attract and retain talent. Companies are used to balancing the costs of such initiatives against the benefits, and programs that support the continued employment of people with criminal records are no different. While I will share examples that I have seen work, these represent a menu of potential choices only. Providing every single one of these options is not required to have a successful program.

DAN MEYER: THE CASE STUDY

On January 28, 2020, Harvard Business School published a case study unlike any in the history of the school or of any business school. Titled "Nehemiah Mfg Co.: Providing a Second Chance," it is the first study of a for-profit company dedicated to providing second chance employment, and Dan Meyer is its CEO, founder, and visionary.[2]

A Cincinnati native with a long track record of success in consumer goods, Dan could easily have rested on his laurels after selling his previous company. However, Dan had an idea for a next company that would operate profitably in manufacturing consumer goods, but in some way give back to his city that was challenged by racial tensions, crime, and deep poverty. In 2009, Dan founded Nehemiah, named after the leader in the Bible who rebuilt the walls of Jerusalem and called the Jewish people to lead moral lives. For Dan, this meant opening his facility in a struggling neighborhood and looking to hire locally. He only started consciously opening his doors to people with felony convictions in 2011 at the request of a local nonprofit. And it didn't work.

Dan was one of the very first second chance employers I met, and it was my visit to their facility in September 2015 that convinced me that second chance hiring was a business proposition. Nehemiah still stands out as one of the most comprehensive examples of "safety net capitalism." This is a phrase I use to describe a different social contract between employer and employee, one in which the holistic support of worker welfare is exchanged for loyal and dedicated workers. Today, roughly 130 of their 180 employees are second chance hires, and unless they cannot otherwise fill a technical need, all their hires are internal. But it was not always so at Nehemiah.

Like others who followed the Undifferentiated Model of second chance hiring, Nehemiah found that hiring people with records delivered erratic results. Dan likes to say that his "aha moment" was when he hired a social worker to support those hires in addressing concerns that had been disrupting their ability to work. The focus on wraparound services through partnerships with outside nonprofits and government agencies dramatically reduced turnover. When I first met Dan, he told me: "I don't have HR people. I have social workers," and I thought he was being figurative—he was not. The firm now employs a team of three social workers, and wraparound services include housing support, micro loans, trainers, and workout facility access. Nehemiah also works hard to build a healthy sense of community for its workforce, with family events and outings.

For all his passion, this is business, not charity, and Dan remains grounded in the sort of fact-based analytics that I learned to expect from Wharton grads like him. His turnover is a fraction of industry averages, and he estimates that associated cost savings and productivity increases dropped an additional 5.2 percent to his cash flow (EBITDA), a huge pickup in a mature industry. Rather than follow a traditional model of using these gains to increase short-term returns to investors or executive compensation, Dan confesses that he reinvests those funds to further support his employees.

Although now moved to a long-established independent workforce development organization, Dan founded the Beacon of Hope Business Alliance, a nonprofit dedicated to showing other companies how to hire people with records and other marginalized workers. This has led to the Greater Cincinnati region becoming one of the hotbeds of True Second Chance hiring. Most recently, this included successful work with Kroger, the national grocery store chain and one of the nation's largest employers. Beyond the local community, Dan travels to share his work, speaking on panels for me and others (he always refuses any compensation, even the reimbursement of travel costs). His work was featured in the January 25, 2020 edition of the *Wall Street Journal*, and now is a subject of a Harvard Business School case study that can inspire generations of future business leaders.

The Candidate Selection Process:
Building a Talent Pipeline

Successful second chance employers find out who is truly ready for employment by having others tell them. The heart of a successful second chance candidate selection process is the referral network. The advantages of referrals are no secret to employers. A 2017 LinkedIn[3] survey of talent acquisition professionals identified employee referrals as the largest source of quality hires. From the business standpoint, referrals from existing employees save time and money in the talent acquisition process. They also have better retention, at least as long as the referring employee is at the company (more on this later).

Internal referrals are valued because the sponsoring employee understands the cultural and skill fit needed to succeed, and because the sponsor essentially vouches for the character of the candidate. A bad candidate reflects negatively on the sponsor, which instills discipline in the referral process. No employee wants the repercussions of injecting a bad employee into the workplace.

Second chance candidates are also best sourced from referral networks. Done right, these networks can provide the critical vetting of character that parallels that which takes place in employee referrals. Just as your own workers refer people with whom they have built a relationship sufficient to have confidence in the candidate's fit and character, second chance referrers do the same in successful models. In fact, understanding the reputational and other risks associated with hiring people with criminal records, it is fair to say that the role of second chance referrers, when properly performed, is even more critical.

The models of successful second chance employment that rely on outside referrals have identified two factors that lead to success: 1) Referrers must have had sufficient time with a person with a criminal record to have built a strong relationship, and 2) They must understand the needs of the employer.

There are numerous potential partners for businesses that want to implement True Second Chance Models. There is a vast array of nonprofit organizations that work with people in need of second chances. In particular, many focus on serving people coming out of incarceration. With more than six hundred thousand people leaving US prisons each year, this is a potentially rich pool of applicants. There are also government organizations that can provide a potential initial screen, attesting to a candidate's readiness for work.

The business owner trying to build a pipeline of quality candidates will not need to rely solely on nonprofit referrals. Companies that have established a reputation as a true second chance employer inevitably attract candidates with criminal records simply because there are so few like-minded enterprises. Some companies will still prefer the vetting provided by a nonprofit partner while others will develop sufficient experience to feel comfortable relying solely on their own judgment and screening process. Nonetheless, the majority of successful second chance employers start with nonprofit referrals.

Building Block #1:
Finding the Right Nonprofit Partner

Employers will have to invest time to identify partners with whom they can work. Most employers will want to have several ongoing relationships with nonprofits, as more employee-referral opportunities are generally better than fewer. Some of these organizations are local, only serving a specific neighborhood, for example, so companies with multiple locations may need to build a network within each geography.

There is no simple directory of organizations that work with people with criminal records, even though there are an abundance of such nonprofits. One good starting point is to identify the closest American Job Center. These are federally funded offices administered by local Workforce Development Boards mandated by the Workforce Innovation and Opportunity Act. They offer free services to job-seekers. Of the nearly 2,400 centers, 1,375 are considered "comprehensive" and will have partner resources on-site, including some nonprofits that focus on reentry.[4] These centers are also the conduit for certain types of second chance employer subsidies discussed later in detail in the following chapter.

A simple Google search of "reentry programs in . . . ," inserting the name of the county or nearest city, will turn up many resources, councils, and organizations that can potentially help. National social service providers like Goodwill have excellent reentry-focused programs in many areas of the country. Local organizations can be as effective as larger groups, in part because they have high levels of accountability to the communities and employers with which they work. Local churches and other faith-based organizations often have their own reentry programs or have a relationship with them. Parole and probation departments in your locality may also be able to point you to effective resources. Whether you work with local, regional, or national organizations, there is value in finding ones located near you. As we'll discuss further, transportation is often a challenge for second chance hires, so finding a nonprofit that serves a population with easier access to your facility may be more fruitful.

Identifying organizations is only half the battle. Selecting which is the right one for you is highly subjective. In my experience, the nonprofit world does not always share the same perspective as the business owner, and many of these organizations see their missions as exclusively serving the immediate needs of their "clients," the people in their programs, to the exclusion of other stakeholders— and by "other stakeholders," I mean you, the potential employer of their clients. I have heard of several instances of nonprofits sending candidates who were not "the most ready," or even ready to be a viable worker at all, but rather were "most in need." If a nonprofit is not willing to be selective in who they refer to you or unwilling to make that selectivity based on your business needs, they are not the partner that can help you build a successful second chance employment program.

There are a number of other factors that are worth considering. Again, no organization will "check all the boxes," but at a minimum, in order for you to be a good partner to them, you should understand their resources and perspectives. Some questions to ask:

▶ **Does the leadership have private sector experience or a focus on understanding the needs of the business community?** A small but noticeable number of people engaged in criminal justice reform, including some in reentry organizations, are frankly hostile to the free enterprise system. It's hard to form a solid partnership with someone who thinks you are the enemy! Much more common is that the staff of these organizations simply have a different set of life experiences. While such diversity of outlooks brings an important perspective to this human resource management issue, it can create barriers to mutual understanding and communication. A truly innovative reentry nonprofit, Project Return, based in Nashville, Tennessee, has established business-friendly teams to bridge this gap.

▶ **How are they funded?** Organizations that are wholly funded by private donations may be more responsive to the needs of the business community, but they also may need to devote more energy to fundraising. Government-funded entities can be effective allies in working through some of the regulatory concerns that can come up in second chance hiring. Again, there is no right or wrong, but having a better understanding of your critical partner makes a better alliance.

▶ **Is success measured by the placement of the candidate or by the candidate's long-term success?** The Cara Program, a workforce development nonprofit in Chicago, does not consider a client a "graduate" until he or she has been gainfully employed for a full year. Measuring success in number of placements doesn't make a nonprofit a bad referral source, but it may reflect the willingness of that nonprofit to devote resources to following up with hires (you may want a different nonprofit for this support anyway), and you may want to reinforce your need for the job-ready candidate, not just a candidate.

▶ **Can they be a policy researcher and advocate for the business community?** Chicago's Safer Foundation takes an active role in policy formation and policy research. In conjunction with the National Employment Law Project, it created an industry-specific guide for healthcare employers and is exploring other industries for which to create similar tools.

▶ **What kind of follow-up do they do with the employer?** Will there be on-site or even telephone follow-up to help address any issues that might arise with the employee?

▶ **Is there an ongoing relationship and mentoring after placement?** The Redemption Project, a Minnesota reentry nonprofit, has taken mentoring to a whole new level, enlisting prospective employers as mentors who begin the process six months before release. Their mentoring curriculum even includes opportunities for employers to introduce norms associated with individual company cultures, enhancing the prospects for successful reentry.

▶ **Do they work collaboratively with law enforcement?** Given the role that parole and probation officers can play in the lives of people with criminal records, nonprofits that can partner with law enforcement bring another dimension of support to the table. The Las Vegas nonprofit Hope for Prisoners has an eighteen-month mentoring program, with many of the volunteer community mentors coming from law enforcement. Part of their programming includes sessions aimed at healing the relationship between justice-involved individuals, communities, and law enforcement. In 2020, President Trump publicly pardoned the organization's founder, convicted bank robber Jon Ponder, in the presence of Ponder's good friend, the FBI agent who had arrested him.

▶ **Do they help build community?** Executive Lloyd Martin introduced second chance hiring to his employer, CKS Packaging, and within three years the company went from five initial hires to more than two hundred, roughly 10 percent of its workforce. Lloyd stresses that reentry, providing a person with ongoing and supported employment, may be insufficient, and that true success also relies on "reintegration." Those who had been led to crime because of unhealthy environments and associates may need reintegration into a whole new community that will support their efforts to build a better life. This is a hard mission for many nonprofits, which have to allocate their limited resources to traditional training programming. Even within these, some distinguish themselves by trying to build community through alumni gatherings and open-door policies for graduates who need additional advice. Building community is an area where faith-based reentry organizations often excel. A faith-based nonprofit cited by many western Michigan companies as an effective partner, 70x7 Life Recovery, has even launched an initiative for families of the incarcerated, ensuring that an intergenerational cycle of incarceration does not persist and supporting the family as a core structure in successful reintegration.

In any successful partnership, setting appropriate expectations is critical to success. The divide that often exists between the viewpoint of for-profit businesses and nonprofit agencies makes this communication critical. Businesses engaging in second chance hiring have every right to expect that referrals be people who are "ready," with the critical understanding that readiness should be measured in terms of a commitment to be a good employee, colleague, and person, but not necessarily experienced in negotiating the everyday challenges of a workplace: you are seeking "diamonds in the rough," not fine-cut gems. If you have business metrics for a successful hire (e.g., lower turnover rates, attendance characteristics), communicate these.

This communication should flow both ways. Nonprofits can help guide employers in what should be reasonable expectations for the types of candidates they can provide. Critically, they may be able to provide insight into areas of patience and forbearance you should show toward the "unpolished" second chance employee. As we will discuss in the next section, accommodations often take the form of patience, the recognition that a second chance hire may not have had the most basic experience with workplace etiquette, raising issues to a supervisor, how to handle family emergencies, and so on. The non-profit partner can help acclimate the employer and serve as a sounding board for appropriate accommodations.

Of course, businesses that expect nonprofits to behave as true partners should also reciprocate. There are many ways that businesses can "pay back" a nonprofit that assists in supporting their staffing needs. The most obvious, of course, is through funding, sharing some of the savings you reap from lower turnover or lower recruiting costs. Just as you expect the nonprofit to listen and respond to your business's needs, you should ask them about their organizational wish list. Some mission-driven organizations could greatly benefit from the types of administrative and operational (budgeting, planning, etc.) acumen that are hallmarks of most successful businesses. Board representation and unofficial or official advisory roles are all ways that businesses can become involved and support their nonprofit partners. Even nonprofits that don't need financial support (typically those that rely heavily on government funding) can use friends and allies.

Finally, the best nonprofits in this space are driven by the mission to help people rebuild their lives. To do this, they need companies that are willing to look beyond the mistakes their clients have made. Nothing is more powerful for their mission than second chance employers who are willing to share their success publicly. When your company has found the advantages of incorporating such hires into your workforce, don't keep it a secret! The instincts of the business community might argue to horde this knowledge as a competitive advantage, but second chance employers should think more strategically. Ultimately, nonprofits will refer the best candidates to those who help them fulfill their mission, which includes spreading the word. Some employers may choose not to advertise that their staff includes people with records, for example, because of the risk to the company's reputation. But even they can serve their nonprofit partners as confidential references. Finally, the benefits to the economy and to our communities from the widespread adoption of second chance hiring are so great that the benefits of sharing this information outweigh any short-term competitive advantage.

Alternative Talent Pipelines

Nonprofit workforce development and reentry-focused nonprofits are among the most common referral sources for candidates with criminal records. However, they are not the only source for employers. As with traditional nonprofits, there is value in trying a variety of referral sources.

The criminal justice system is a potential resource for candidate referrals. In some jurisdictions, there is far less passion for rehabilitation than for other traditional purposes of sentencing: retribution (punishment), incapacitation (taking offenders off the streets), and deterrence. Fortunately, leaders within the criminal justice system— those who administer the courts, prosecutors, jails, prisons, and offices of parole and probation, right up to state attorneys general and federal authorities—are all coming to see that rehabilitation is one of the best guarantees of public safety.

Within the court system, diversion programs offer alternatives to incarceration. Typically, these are "drug courts" where offenders are

put under the supervision of a court and provided with support services. Such programs can offer an appealing referral resource for employers: to be eligible for these diversion programs, participants have
usually been through a screening program that deems them a low risk
to public safety and good candidates for rehabilitation. Moreover,
they are already being provided with support services while under the
court's supervision, which typically includes drug testing. Philadelphia's MENTOR court-based program (see Chapter Two) also provides an additional layer of community mentors who can provide
ongoing support even after the court's formal role ends. That mentorship piece is important since the downside of working with diversion programs tends to be the downside of working with young
drug offenders—the risk that they slide back into the same environment that got them into trouble initially.

Moving up the scale of supervision, local jails can sometimes be a
resource. While incarceration in jails tend to be of short and unpredictable periods, some sheriff's offices are looking to develop employment and education programs for the people under their supervision.
In the basement of Chicago's Cook County Jail, chef Bruno Abate
has established a pizza kitchen under his Recipe for Change program.
Many of these programs are short-lived and may not have time to
teach hard skills that are of measurable value to employers, nor do the
people running these programs always have time to establish a basis
for providing references to employers. However, individuals released
from jail sentences are generally in for pretrial detention and have
been released because they are deemed to be minor threats to public
safety or have completed short sentences for relatively minor crimes.
The voluntary participation in these programs can build "soft skills"
that will support employment success and may reflect a desire for a
better life by the participant.

Prisons, where inmates serve longer sentences, can give officials the opportunity to assess readiness for employment. This is particularly true when prisons offer strong vocational training programs, have work-release programs, or, in certain instances, in-prison work. Beyond formal training programs, evidence that inmates used their time to improve themselves through education or rehabilitative curricula like the Reaching Out from Within program (described in Chapter Two) also suggests better job candidates.

Prison labor programs tend to be painted with a broad and negative brush, but it is critical to note that all such programs are not the same. Just as there are systems of hiring people after incarceration that build human capital (the True Second Chance Model) and those that do not (the Disposable Employee Model), the same is true of employment behind bars. At its worst, labor in prison bears a striking resemblance to slavery—it can be compulsory (enforced by punishment for refusal to participate), offer few of the protections provided to others under labor laws, and the pay can be as little as pennies per day. Further sustaining the slavery analogy, it is permitted under an exemption found within the Thirteenth Amendment; the thirty-two words of the first section expressly forbid slavery and involuntary servitude, but for a fourteen-word exclusion: "except as a punishment for crime whereof the party shall have been duly convicted."

Prison officials note that some of this labor (laundry, food preparation, etc.) is related to maintaining the operations of a place where residents receive room and board at the expense of taxpayers, and higher pay would only increase the cost of incarceration to the public, historically something with limited political support. Prison work—keeping inmates engaged and active—is also believed to assist in in-prison safety, both for guards and prisoners.

More complicated and, for many, morally questionable is the outsourcing of cheap prison labor for the benefit of private sector companies. This practice has been long established in the federal prison system through Unicor (formerly known as the Federal Prison Industries). Even beyond the ethical issues, businesses using this program must consider reputation risk, but this may provide a potential source of trained labor. Whatever the source of an inmate's training, the act of hiring people from incarceration and embracing their career through the True Second Chance Model is not morally ambiguous—it is an unadulterated good for employees and the community.

A LOOK AT ZEPHYR PRODUCTS, INC.

Some of the longest running work-release programs in the country operate in Leavenworth, Kansas. In 1979, visionary businessman Fred Braun started what would become a small hub of manufacturing companies that rely on work-release labor from a nearby state prison. Braun, now deceased, was inspired by his belief that "work is the greatest rehabilitator of all."

Zephyr Products, Inc., one of these businesses, is now owned by CEO Randy Reinhart, who has continued and expanded upon Braun's work. Of their 110 employees, roughly 80 are inmate workers. The facility looks no different than any of the other manufacturing plants I have visited over the years. There are no guards or fences, just a clean and well-lit facility.

Zephyr, the oldest of the three businesses that operate the work-release programs in Leavenworth, has employed more than a thousand inmates over the years, although some were removed along the way. A common reason for an inmate to lose employment is possession of contraband—typically, tobacco products. Job candidates are selected based on "attitude" and often have been through in-prison rehabilitation nonprofit programs like Reaching Out from Within and Brothers in Blue Reentry. The average tenure with the company is eighteen months. During their time, in addition to solid wages, many earn industry-accepted welding and forklift certifications as well as the valued skills associated with that piece of paper. While Zephyr prefers that its workers get outside experience upon prison release, some do come back as managers and senior workers. The success of their 351 "alumni" is stunning. As of December 31, 2019, the three-year recidivism rate was 2 percent.

The prospective second chance employer should not be too quick to dismiss partnering with prison officials in any way that supports some of these programs. It is important to note that some in-prison employment initiatives pay rates that are not exploitative and play a vital role in rehabilitation and job readiness. In fact, some private companies operating within prison resemble the True Second Chance Model in the holistic embrace of their workers. These programs, while relatively few, can be important partners in developing potential employees. Televerde, a private sector company headquartered in Phoenix, operates call centers in women's correctional facilities in Arizona and Indiana (Televerde also has call centers outside of prisons). They pay market wages including overtime and offer pay raises and college credit for their training programs. It is impressive that roughly one hundred employees in their headquarters originally came from the prison programs and include senior managers.

Any employer who either transports goods produced by inmates across state lines or sells them to the federal government must operate under the Prison Industry Enhancement Certification Program

(PIECP). Although there have been some criticisms of the rigor of the oversight of the program, PIECP requires that workers be reimbursed at "prevailing" wages, a pay rate above minimum wage, and often much higher. In these cases, there are allowable levels of deductions to defray some of the costs of incarceration, paying taxes, family support, and victim restitution. The bottom line: inmates walk away with job experience and money in the bank, both of which are sources of stabilization upon release.

Work-release programs offer a variation on a prison labor force, but one with highly constructive outcomes and far fewer ethical questions. Inmates are allowed to leave the grounds of their facilities to work for a private-sector employer. While they must return each night, these programs offer a valuable transition to life after incarceration and pay fairly. There are screens as to which inmates are allowed to participate, certain levels of supervision are retained even during the workday, and not all participants complete these programs. From the standpoint of the future employer, successful completion (not just participation) in a work-release program not only may provide needed hard skills, but also indicates a high level of job readiness after release.

Also promising is the growth of in-prison vocational training programs that can provide a pipeline of talent to employers. Among the most notable projects are Michigan's Vocational Villages. These are training centers currently established at two men's facilities with a third scheduled to open at a women's facility. Originally built around skilled trades, the program is notable for its interest in partnering with the private sector. The trainers have generally come from trade unions and have extensive private sector experience. DTE Electric Company (formerly known as Detroit Edison Company) recently worked with the Michigan Department of Corrections to create a custom training program at one Village to sustain the ranks of 1,300 tree trimmers needed to keep power lines clear throughout its footprint. Like most work-release programs, there are hurdles to participating in the training, and strict enforcement of rules to stay enrolled—successful completion and certifications are a good signal to post-release employers of worthy job candidates.

Although the Vocational Villages were built to train for traditional jobs, they are expanding into computer coding in partnership with the California nonprofit The Last Mile. This organization has been leading the way in establishing in-prison training programs for the information economy.

Of course, there are post-release training programs that train to different skills. Perhaps none is more ambitious—or successful—than EDWINS Leadership & Restaurant Institute in Cleveland, Ohio, the brainchild of Brandon Chrostowski, already an accomplished chef and restaurant manager when he founded EDWINS in 2007. With few exceptions, the enrolled students are drawn from the ranks of the formerly incarcerated for a six-month intensive curriculum in the restaurant and hospitality business, learning everything from classic French cooking techniques to bookkeeping. The program offers comprehensive wraparound support that allows students to achieve stability while they build their skills, including a stipend, on-campus housing, and an active partnership with other social service providers for additional services. Students have the opportunity to hone their skills in the attached high-end classic French restaurant, which has earned its solid five-star rating on Yelp. As of 2019, the program had 301 graduates—and only two had recidivated, an astonishingly low rate. The quality of its graduates can be seen in other measures: the Institute has a waiting list of interested employers, its graduates work in more than ninety restaurants, and some of the top-rated restaurants in the area have had such a positive experience that they employ as many as five EDWINS graduates. The program has become so successful that it has expanded to in-prison programs, a butcher shop, and a bakery.

While programs with training as advanced as EDWINS are relatively rare, many cities have transitional employment programs that provide intentionally temporary work, but also offer the opportunity to build basic work-readiness. Among the most prominent national organizations is the Center for Employment Opportunities (CEO), which has become the largest reentry employer in the nation. Currently in ten states and twenty-eight cities, the program can be a great resource for second chance employers. The process begins with a weeklong job-readiness curriculum and then participants go to work on crews providing supplemental maintenance and beautification projects. During this period, participants are continuously assessed, coached, and provided with job search and placement assistance. Critically, CEO continues to support the employment of its participants even after they have been placed,

Like other workforce development programs targeting those in need of a second chance, there are great local providers of transitional employment as well. One of my earliest research forays was to the North Lawndale Employment Network (NLEN) in Chicago. Like CEO and others, the program offers broad support services and coaching, but the primary transitional employment is beekeeping and the manufacture of honey and honey-infused cosmetics. NLEN was founded by Brenda Palms-Barber, a recipient of one of the MacArthur Foundation's new Creative and Effective Institutions awards, which are similar to its so-called "genius grants," but intended for up-and-coming nonprofits.

Many employers have basic but important expectations for entry-level employees: show up on time, dress appropriately, and act responsibly. Like all good workforce development programs, NLEN strictly enforces attendance, drug testing, and other rules, but as I often joke with audiences, the bees no doubt provide immediate feedback to the beekeepers who fail to dress or act appropriately. The success of NLEN's program is no joke, however; according to its latest website update, of more than five hundred individuals, less than 10 percent have recidivated, and three out of four have improved their income, net worth, and FICO score.[5] Like other transitional employers, NLEN provides a valuable talent pipeline to employers.

Entrepreneurship training programs for people with records and for the recently incarcerated can also be thought of as a form of workforce development program and potential referral partners. While the goal of these programs is to create successful entrepreneurs, we all know that most entrepreneurial ventures fail. For returning citizens, the drive and grit and conviction that "necessity is the mother of invention" indeed produces some great successes, but this is also a population that typically lacks access to capital and credit as well as having a limited network. Someone trained to think like a business owner, however, can make a terrific employee. Programs like the Pivot Program at Georgetown University or the great work and advocacy of the Brian Hamilton Foundation's Inmates to Entrepreneurs program absolutely elevate the business skills of their participants.

For some employers, partnering with staffing agencies offers a chance to "test out" potential second chance hires who have been sourced elsewhere. Beyond that, a variation on transitional employers is staffing agencies that focus on hiring people with records and placing them in temporary assignments with employers. MaineWorks is a for-profit company (a Certified B Corporation) founded by Margo Walsh. Walsh, a former Goldman Sachs and Hewitt professional and recovering alcoholic, was inspired to create MaineWorks while volunteering in the local Cumberland County Jail's prerelease center, giving talks on recovery. She has built relationships with companies in the Portland area, many of which came to trust that she appropriately vets the people she sends to their job sites.

Cornbread Hustle is another for-profit, second chance staffing agency in Dallas. Founded in 2016 by Cheri Garcia, the agency provides employers with the option of temp-to-hire. Many of their workers are sourced from workforce development and reentry nonprofits, and the organization drug tests workers. Her workers also have access to an in-house "resiliency expert," who can provide coaching through work challenges or personal trauma. Cornbread Hustle shares the faith-based inspiration that appears among many of the second chance employment leaders. Cheri told me: "We like to see ourselves as kingdom builders. We solve all of our problems using the Bible."

Nonprofit staffing agencies dedicated to second chance staffing also exist. Founded in Atlanta in 2007, First Step Staffing provides not only job opportunities, but transportation and, critically, coaching. The organization entered the staffing arena in 2015 through the purchase of a traditional for-profit agency, and used that base of relationship and infrastructure to convert to its current mission. This acquisition strategy has allowed First Step to expand to Philadelphia, Nashville, Orlando, Duluth, Los Angeles, and two other California locations. Similar organizations, both nonprofit and for-profit, exist in many major cities, and all offer a potential pipeline to second chance hires.

Finally, beyond those who provide transitional work are organizations that provide transitional housing for people leaving incarceration. The best of these can be valuable referral sources, particularly those that provide broad support services, are willing to be discerning in who they recommend for employment, and have a follow-up program to sustain that employment. The largest provider to the federal prison system is a Louisville-based nonprofit, Dismas Charities, which operates thirty-six facilities (one of which is nonresidential) in twelve states. As with transitional employers, local interim housing providers are also important options for employers looking for partners. In Chicago, St. Leonard's Ministries is a nonprofit that oversees St. Leonard's House (for men) and Grace House (for women), providing not only housing, but extensive services, education, and training for participants. There are also for-profit housing providers. For those employers who want to offer second chances to people who have battled addiction, parallel organizations exist: Lexington, Kentucky, restaurateur Rob Perez called such addiction halfway houses his "staffing agencies." As with other types of potential referral networks, there is no one-size-fits-all provider. Finding a good fit for a single company's staffing needs requires due diligence and the creation of an effective working partnership at the local level.

Building Block #2: Employee Support Process

A good referral network can produce good hires, but sometimes being a good hire is not enough. Scholar Emilio Castilla argues that one reason candidates referred by other employees have historically had success is that they have a resource to assist them with onboarding and mentoring—the employee who referred them.[6] Referrals who come in through outside networks also benefit from systems of support and specific accommodations. Such systems are critical for successful second chance programs.

"Support" and "employee accommodations" sound costly to the business ear, but most businesses have been doing this for years to attract other demographics. Among the accommodations:

- ▶ Family leave, adoption, and fertility treatment policies to attract young and potential parents
- ▶ Bereavement policies
- ▶ Health/dental/vision plans (even pre–Affordable Care Act requirements, these were found in the majority of businesses)
- ▶ 401(k) matches for mid- and late-career workers saving for retirement
- ▶ The foosball/Ping-Pong/pool table or video game room for the millennial employees
- ▶ Relocating to urban core environments to attract millennial employees and tech talent

Not one of these policies was free. Every single one came with a dollar cost, and often a substantial one. Most of these would have seemed like foolish expenditures a few short decades ago, but now have become necessities as the race for talent heats up. Looking forward ten to twenty years, when the baby boom generation will be largely out of the workforce, the millennials will be fully in, and businesses will truly feel the sting of the decline in birth rates following the 1990 cyclical peak. What accommodations that seem far-fetched today will be commonplace then? The point is not to focus solely on the cost of these programs, but rather on the return on that investment.

What types of issues do people with records face that may need accommodation? The most obvious are obligations that may be related to the terms of probation or parole. Second chance employers have related stories of parole officers disrupting work. One CEO in Philadelphia described a parole officer arriving for a routine check-in dressed in what he described as "full S.W.A.T. gear." Other employers have shared stories of parole officers who resisted allowing second chance employees to work at sites out of state, or to meet at hours consistent with their employer's demands. Often this is because parole officers have become habituated to saying "no," or they must deal with potential career repercussions if flexibility were to ever result in a public safety risk, or they don't realize that they have a true partner in a second chance employer. This can be fixed. John Koufos, the national director of reentry initiatives at Right on Crime and executive director of Safe Streets & Second Chances, advises that employers "meet with the chief probation officer in the jurisdiction and tell him or her exactly what you are looking for in an employee. Tell them what your work hours are and confirm that they will not interrupt your workday unless absolutely necessary." Koufos, a former attorney before his own mistake and incarceration, holds an unusual distinction; he is the only attorney to have argued a case on behalf of a client before the New Jersey Supreme Court while out on bail himself, and to learn of the disposition while he was in prison (he won).

JEFFREY BROWN: GROCER TO THE FOOD DESERTS

Jeff is the founder, CEO, and president of Brown's Super Stores, one the country's top small grocery store chains with annual sales of $500 million across twelve stores. He's also a second chance employer and an innovator, bringing both economic and nutritional help to the communities in which he operates.

Among the many challenges facing poor neighborhoods is the absence of easily accessible fresh produce and quality food stores, dubbed "food deserts." A 2012 USDA study reports, "Relative to all other census tracts, food desert tracts tend to have . . . higher rates of abandoned or vacant homes, and residents who have lower levels of education, lower incomes, and higher unemployment."[7]

"People told me you couldn't profitably operate a quality supermarket in these neighborhoods. I knew they were wrong—my great-grandfather operated a corner store, and my grandfather ran a grocery store in Philadelphia." Jeff is a fourth-generation grocer, the son of an operator of supermarkets in New Jersey, and he was willing to take a chance.

In 2004, Jeff defied conventional wisdom and opened his first store in a low-income Philadelphia neighborhood. The store was successful and is now one of six stores he operates in what had previously been food deserts. Jeff attributes his accomplishment to creating strong bonds with the communities where his stores are located, and that includes hiring locally. It was at one of his public meetings that an attendee challenged him to include second chance hiring—she argued that, "When we have jobs, your business does better." Jeff agreed, in turn challenging his team to start with six employees with records. Today, 600 of the 2,500 employees of Brown's Super Stores are second chance hires, including many in management positions.

Like many other successful second chance employers, Jeff found that he needed a workforce-development nonprofit that would meet his specific needs. In 2009, he founded the nonprofit Uplift Solutions, which expanded into different programs including workforce development. Uplift provides training, wraparound solutions, including coordinating with probation and parole officers (who have become valued referral sources). The nonprofit houses social workers who partner with employers and provide ongoing support to graduates. The success of Brown's Super Stores has inspired other business leaders to follow Jeff's lead. Not only does Uplift supply workers to Brown's, it also creates a talent pipeline for other businesses and for competitors of Brown's Super Stores.

Many of the second chance employers with whom I've worked are in manufacturing and other businesses where employees have limited interaction with the public. Not so at Brown's, where most roles are customer-facing. I asked Jeff about any adverse customer reaction. He told me that his second chance hiring is actually a positive for customers in his urban stores—they understand what this type of employment means for their community. He also believes that a tight relationship with the neighborhood has his customers looking out for his business, reducing costs due to "shrinkage," the industry euphemism for inventory losses that include damage and shoplifting. He admits that he is quieter about his second chance hiring at his suburban locations, but his leadership in this area is no secret.

Jeff shared his admiration for a consistent trait among his second chance hires: grit. When I last spoke with Jeff, the COVID-19 pandemic continued to rage, and many employers found that 30 percent of their workforce did not want to come in. But this wasn't an issue for Brown's workforce: "They're accustomed to challenges that others are not and are prepared to manage through risks." Even as unemployment levels soared, and Jeff could have his pick of workers, he emphasized, "That has not changed my hiring practices at all."

Most accommodations that second chance employees may require have nothing to do with their criminal record and everything to do with poverty. The vast majority of successful second chance employers have shared that recognizing these needs is the most critical element to successful second chance hiring. They have also found that support mechanisms originally intended for second chance hires have benefited a much broader component of their workforce, with a positive impact on retention and turnover costs. What are the needs of those caught in the deep poverty so often associated with, but not exclusive to, a past criminal conviction? The basics: housing, transportation, and even food. Beyond that, employees with limited resources may need assistance with child or elder care, unexpected financial setbacks (e.g., car repairs), or legal assistance.

The list of wraparound services that help maintain employment is daunting. In the majority of cases, the employer is not furnishing this support directly, but rather partnering with nonprofits or simply serving as a referral to nonprofit and government agencies. The same discovery process for finding potential referrers among social service providers will often generate potential support providers, even if they are not one and the same (i.e., you might use one for prospective employee referrals, but partner with another with whom you work to support existing employees).

In western Michigan, twenty companies participate in a shared wraparound service provider called The Source. It is the brainchild of Mark Peters, CEO of food manufacturer Butterball Farms, who felt his company alone did not have sufficient scale to offer the full range of support needed by his second chance hires. Even larger companies would eventually join to take advantage of the efficiencies of shared services; the social work team has regularly scheduled visits to the member companies. Although a nonprofit, The Source is a business proposition. The participating businesses consider this an investment, measuring their return in dollars saved through lower turnover-associated costs. Using an algorithm that ties usage of services to employee retention, The Source has delivered a whopping 219 percent return on funding costs.

The final accommodation that employers should consider is one that does not relate directly to either a criminal record or being mired in poverty: mentoring. Second chance employers quickly realize that they have taken for granted some basic expectations about employment: showing up on time, dressing appropriately, taking coaching or criticism, the need to communicate with a supervisor. These may not have been learned skills in some of the communities that have produced so many people in need of a second chance. To some degree, the right nonprofit referral partners will have addressed some of these gaps, but having mentoring available in the workplace allows both the timely addressing of any deficiencies and helps build the trust between employer and employee so essential to success. People with criminal records can be easily tripped up and leave employment without a coaching relationship.

It is easy to understand how second chance hires could go off track if they lose housing or transportation. The importance of mentorship and trust is not always so obvious to the new second chance employer. One employer shared with me that he almost lost a second chance employee when he was innocently asked in a break room, "So, where did you come from?"—the shame and embarrassment of incarceration and no ready response almost sent the employee out the door for good. Another employer asked a second chance hire to attend a training class at a local community college. The thought of attending a college, even for a single class, was so far outside the employee's life experience and intimidating that he not only did not show up for the class, he simply did not return to work. In both cases, managers acted as mentors and worked with their employees to keep them on track. While these are extreme examples, there are few employees or companies that would not benefit from a strong culture and structure of mentoring.

The degree to which the cost/benefit analysis necessitates this investment also depends on the labor pool. At a program in which I participated, a representative of trade unions in the Los Angeles area that are active second chance employers stated that they did not need to make accommodations and yet were very successful. When people with records have strong families, communities, histories of work, and job-ready skills, these accommodations are not needed. Similarly, someone with a record from the distant past, who had a stable history of work, is just another employee, unlikely to need nontraditional support. Realistically, however, employers seeking the advantages of untapped talent should expect to adapt some of their practices to maximize this opportunity.

Like any other investment, implementing second chance hiring is not risk-free, nor is it cost-free, but it can be cost-effective. Imagine the position of a second chance hire who has never been given a real first chance, who has been acculturated to think of himself as a burden, and who has faced rejection after rejection. You can be the employer who treated that person with dignity, provided opportunity and support. When done right, in the words of Ruben Castillo, a federal judge and a former commissioner of the US Sentencing Commission, "These are exceptional employees, because they are so grateful to be given an opportunity that they will run through a brick wall for you."[8] Those traits of engagement and loyalty become measurable business metrics that translate into low turnover and high productivity.

The fundamental idea of these two processes is simple: find the people who are ready to work and empower them to prosper as contributing employees. Even if there is not a tight labor market as you read these words, successful talent acquisition is a "long game" and our declining birth rates dictate that if labor markets aren't tight now, they will be again. This is the kind of environment where there is a "first mover advantage." Talent will always be in demand. Untapped talent among those with a criminal record is substantial, but not infinite. Those employers who can establish these processes today will not only have the first pick among this talent pool, they will have established a pipeline that will continue to deliver dedicated employees in the tightest of labor markets.

In the next chapter, we'll share the lessons learned from the pioneers of second chance hiring on how to implement and refine this model for your business.

IMPLEMENTATION, CHALLENGES, AND REFINEMENT

They are harder to begin with, but more productive in the end.
— RAY DALTON, *CEO of reLink Medical*
and serial entrepreneur, on second chance hires

L ike many business constructs, the True Second Chance Model (described in Chapter Four) is simpler in concept than execution, but this chapter will break down that implementation process into achievable steps based on the experience of successful business leaders. This chapter starts with a quote from the enormously successful CEO featured in a sidebar in Chapter One as a reminder that this is a business proposition with an investment and a return. The concept of identifying people ready to turn their lives around and then supporting them appropriately makes intuitive sense, but of course "the devil is in the details." Ideas for finding the critical non-profit or government agency partners are in the preceding chapter, while this chapter focuses on what steps the aspiring second chance employer must take internally. There are multiple steps and challenges in this type of hiring, but there is a payoff. A friend, a long-time expert in commercializing technology, heard me lay out the data on the advantages of second chance hiring and suggested that this book should be subtitled, "A Solution to Finding Grateful, Loyal, and Qualified Employees." Consider this chapter the how-to manual of that "solution."

The Leader's Role: Building the Vision

Successful second chance employers consistently have one thing in common—a leader who champions the development of this hiring. Like any disruption to the status quo, successful implementation requires a leader who must not only be prepared to face down the traditional inertia inherent in any enterprise, but articulate a specific positive vision and overcome legitimate objections. Whether that is a formal mission or vision statement, a statement of purpose, or just well understood common ground, implementing second chance hiring will be more difficult without this bedrock belief system.

Some business leaders have created a vision autonomously. Others may have learned of this in business school or through corporate training. There are abundant resources to assist executives in uncovering, refining, and building a common purpose in a company, from consultants to websites to TED Talks to books from every decade. Students of management will recognize the names of authors like the late Peter Drucker and Jim Collins who have written on this subject. Currently, Simon Sinek is among the best-known proponents of the power of vision, following a popular 2009 TED Talk and the 2009 publication of his first book, *Start with Why*.

The better this vision can be articulated, the better it can pervade the organization. The more that second chance hiring can be tied to that vision, the easier the path forward. Many businesses do not have a clear vision, but my experience with successful second chance employers is that they are among those who do. I suspect this is a mix of causation and correlation; while a vision helps with the implementation of second chance hiring, I believe that the same spirit of innovation that causes leaders to develop and embrace a corporate vision also drives interest in hiring marginalized workers. Ray Dalton's company PartsSource was the first to develop an online catalog in its field; Jeff Brown's ShopRite stores served urban food deserts and helped inspire First Lady Michelle Obama's nutrition campaign (Jeff was recognized at President Obama's first State of the Union address); Skender, a Chicago-based construction firm, is pioneering high-design, affordable, manufactured housing; Brian Hamilton, whose foundation trains returning citizens, built Sageworks, the country's first fintech company—the list goes on and on.

Social enterprises, public beneficial corporations, and Certified B Corps are the "low-hanging fruit" as candidates for becoming second chance employers. These are organizations that already have a built-in vision that is likely to be friendly to the concept of hiring marginalized workers. These are mission-driven enterprises that go beyond a purely profit-driven focus and commit to purpose, accountability, and transparency. Social enterprises are generally nonprofits with a purpose-driven business, while beneficial corporations are for-profits that have elected to organize under laws available in thirty states (and Washington, DC). Regardless of legal status, corporations may choose to qualify as a Certified B Corporation, a designation administered by the nonprofit B Lab. One other variant, the L3C, or "low-profit, limited liability company," structure is available in a handful of states, offering a mission-oriented structure somewhat similar to LLCs (limited liability corporations).

It is no accident that Michigan-based Cascade Engineering, mentioned elsewhere in this chapter and again in Chapter Seven, is not only one of the world's largest B Corps, but also has one of the best and longest established second chance programs in the country. Cascade has built its culture around what the company calls a "triple bottom line," consisting of a commitment to People, Planet, and Profit (and listed in that order). With this bedrock, Cascade built out its Welfare to Career initiative. This program informed many of the best practices that have guided this work, provided careers and futures for hundreds of people with criminal records, and inspired other companies in its home base of western Michigan to implement second chance hiring.

Of course, many companies self-identify as purpose-driven organizations, whether or not they adopt any kind of official status. One common such identification that I have seen among second chance employers is a religious orientation, particularly one focused on Christianity. The concepts of original sin, forgiveness, and redemption that compose much of the Christian message are, of course, well suited to a willingness to hire people who have transgressed the law.

When a business leader with a social or religious vision that has not been inculcated throughout the organization, there are pitfalls in trying to implement second chance hiring. One terrific CEO with whom I have collaborated had deeply held Christian beliefs and had committed to giving second chances, placing those with criminal records among his thousands of employees. Unfortunately, some of his executive team believed that this was an extracurricular crusade that had no place in the business and fought this initiative, blocking progress. Ultimately, this served no one well. The CEO terminated the recalcitrant executives' employment, and his efforts to build a second chance hiring program were held back. At the CEO's request, I brought in the leader of a company with a mature second chance hiring program, and we worked with the new team and a strong reentry nonprofit to reinvigorate the effort.

For those companies without an explicit social or religious purpose, there are plenty of visions that can be tied to second chance hiring and may already be part of the corporate culture. Elements of a positive vision include:

- ▶ Growth: "We can help more customers if we can grow our business, and to grow our business we must grow and invest in our workforce."
- ▶ Innovation: "We are always looking for continuous improvement and new ways to prosper."
- ▶ Community: "We are good citizens, and we're making sure our hiring reflects the totality of our community."
- ▶ Higher purpose: "We are more than a machine for profits—we want to make contributions to the lives of our customers and employees."
- ▶ Talent development: "Our greatest asset is our people— we invest in our people."

All these approaches can be tied to second chance hiring. There are few companies that do not already have a mission or vision that does not have one of the five elements listed above. For the leader, tying this to concrete actions is a way to bring that vision to life and, as such, is a challenge to be embraced.

Communication and Overcoming Objections

In my first significant role as a manager, I was taught early on in my career about my three best friends named Pete: "'peat, 'peat, and repeat." We've all learned that one of the ways that organizations understand priorities and enact change is when the same message is repeated consistently and clearly, almost to the point of pain.

Implementing second chance hiring is no different, and success starts with strong messaging. In the case of this particular initiative, that communication should start at the highest levels of the organization, typically the executive team. The pushback that leaders face in seeking to hire people with criminal records is greater than for most other initiatives and requires that the first round of discussions be limited to a small group with direct accountability to a leader who is willing to drive this change. The concept of having employees and coworkers with a criminal record can prompt a visceral, negative response, and without a disciplined communication strategy, this can become a whirlwind that can derail the project. Several second chance employers reported that they had employees threaten to quit over the prospect of adding people with records to the payrolls. The leadership team itself not only must be won over, it must then deliver a united front and well-thought-out counters to objections.

There is a valid question whether the introduction of second chance hiring needs to be communicated beyond the executive ranks. The business benefit of second chance hiring is typically to establish a pipeline of talent. If this is the case, it inevitably becomes common knowledge, so it's best addressed up front when management can better shape the conversation. Of course, a one-off exception in a firm that does not otherwise hire people with records would not need communication; such communication might even be inappropriate if it effectively broadcasts a new hire's background. Nor would extensive communication necessarily be required in industries where hiring people with records is considered a norm. The restaurant and construction industries come to mind as traditionally felon-friendly fields where hiring people with records is an expected norm. A chef engaged in a second chance training program in Michigan explained to me that, "You can't swing a cat in a restaurant kitchen without hitting a felon!"

Under the assumption that you, the reader of this book, are interested in a scalable pipeline of talent, a broad communication strategy should be anticipated. That strategy begins at the top of the management structures, ready to address potential objections. The pushback of the executive team is likely to not only encompass the concerns of the general employee population but may also include broader corporate issues. Each leader has his or her own style, but engaging executives in crafting a solution could be as simple as asking, "How do you think we could answer that concern?" My hope, of course, is that this book will also be a resource for these discussions.

Companies are generally concerned with four broad issues related to hiring people with records: safety, performance, reputation risk, and legal liability. All these issues represent reasonable fears and deserve respectful, well-thought-out responses. As barriers to creating a second chance hiring program, these are surmountable.

Of these four, safety is typically the first and greatest concern—whether employees, both staff and management, will be safe, and whether customers will be safe. There is a natural tendency to associate a criminal record with the worst and most violent crimes. There are three responses to this objection: 1) reassurance that the leadership shares this concern, 2) education on what it might mean to have a criminal record, and 3) commitment to "going slow" and controlling the hiring criteria.

CEO-owners of family businesses shared with me that they personalized the reassurance of workplace safety, stressing that they, too, wanted to ensure that their sons and daughters would be safe when they came into the business. Whether family-owned or not, leaders must stress that second chance hiring does not mean compromising the safety of the workplace. One of the ways to soften resistance to this is to offer examples (see Chapter One) of ways people could receive a felony conviction. In my own speaking engagements, I have found it productive to talk about examples that people might have experienced from their own youthful mistakes, the mistakes of their children, or the mistakes of people in their community: Did you ever drive drunk? Do drugs? Get into a fight? Our national opioid epidemic has impacted such a broad cross-section of society, so many more people now know someone who has been caught up in the criminal justice system. My question to parents is, "If it were your son or daughter who made a mistake and paid their debt to society, how long should it be held against them?"

Finally, it may be worth reminding colleagues that, throughout their day, they may already be interacting, unknowingly yet happily, with people with criminal records. What do any of us really know about the person who prepares our food, drives our ride-share vehicle, repairs our air conditioner? With nineteen million convicted felons in the United States, we already work with people with criminal records, but just don't know it.

The most effective argument for countering workforce safety concerns is the degree to which employers can control the criteria by which people are eligible for hire. Being open to hiring people with criminal records does not have to mean being open to *all* people with criminal records. Typically, when first implementing second chance hiring, second chance pioneers initially limited their consideration to people who had been convicted of nonviolent offenses. Readers may remember from Chapter Two that, in aggregate, people with nonviolent crimes do not have the lowest recidivism rates—but good, quality people can be found in every instance. Employers typically start with a narrow list of acceptable past offenses and broaden the criteria as they gain positive experience. As with everything related to second chance hiring, retaining flexibility is important. Employers should stress their commitment to workplace safety and not bring in employees who would jeopardize that. However, they should avoid specifically committing to only nonviolent offenses—for example, a violent act committed at age eighteen should not necessarily permanently disqualify someone twenty years later.

Performance concerns are generally associated with public perception rather than reality. Some of the tactics to defuse safety concerns can also deflect fears that people with records simply aren't up to the task. Again, just as with safety, stressing that overall performance standards will not be compromised is an important strategy, although employers should also communicate that there may need to be additional flexibility and coaching early in the process. Second chance employers consistently emphasize the need to retain flexibility in their hiring, coaching, and firing policies while they learn.

It can be trickier to counter a performance-related objection if some on your team had a previous negative experience working with people with records. Often, this is associated with the models of second chance hiring that do not recognize the accommodations needed to support such employees (the Undifferentiated Model or the Disposable Employee Model described in Chapter Four). The overwhelming likelihood is that employees who have directly witnessed disappointing results from hires with records did not have an appropriate talent pipeline, an appropriate support system, or both. "How were prospective second chance hires referred?" and "How were second chance hires supported?" are important questions to ask. This sort of discussion serves to highlight that the True Second Chance Model approaches the challenge differently and consequently produces different—and better—results.

One technique that has worked well for me in countering objections based on safety or performance is to rely on the tool of argument known as *reductio ad absurdum*, taking an opposition argument to an absurd extreme in order to support your point. In practice, this looks something like, "So, are you saying that nobody with a criminal record can be a good employee?" or "Are you saying that every person who made a mistake and has a record is a bad person?" The point of this method is to break the reflexive fear and negativity, and help the person reframe the issues into questions that begin with the word "how": "How can we find the person with a criminal record who will be a good employee?" or "How can we find the person who may have made a mistake, but is a good person?"

Legal liability concerns are not likely to be an issue for the broad employee base, but may well be raised by executives, or the legal and HR professionals on your team. Every employer's worst nightmare is being subject to a negligent hiring lawsuit, where an employee's tortious actions can become the employer's liability if the misdeed was "foreseeable." These civil suits are quite rare, but still a legitimate concern for the second chance employer given the potential cost in terms of money, time, and reputation. A rigorous and well-defined process for candidate selection is, of course, a strong part of the defense. Many states offer some forms of protection to employers of people with records. In states like Texas, some of this is automatic, while in other states, certificates of employability (known by various names, including "provisional pardon") granted to people with records protect their employers if known at the time of hire. Reforms related to this issue are discussed in depth in Chapter Seven along with resources for identifying certain available tools. Employers should consult legal counsel for the available protections in their operating jurisdictions.

Part of an effective internal dialogue with the management team can include third-party partners to demystify the process, and build collaboration between the business and the nonprofit on which it will rely for qualified candidates or support services. Alex Love, HR diversity and inclusion consultant, is also a partner in the reentry initiative of a for-profit consultancy, Envoy Growth. Among her credentials, Alex established a second chance hiring program at Vice Media in New York. She recommends that before launching a pilot, managers and outside agencies should come together for "a closed-door conversation to answer questions, to really understand where they might have certain anxieties, and really better understand the levels of support that we have, and what changes we've made as the employer and our goals around second chance hiring . . . so that you can really prepare those managers to be ready for folks from this background."[1] Some second chance employers provide ongoing training for managers that can include visits to other second chance employers or participation in poverty and reentry simulations.

A separate but equally valid communication decision for the executive team is the degree to which second chance hiring programs should be advertised to the customer base or general public. While each leadership team will have to make its own assessment, there are three criteria that tend to dominate the ultimate choice.

- ▶ How customer-facing are employees? Manufacturing and construction have always been areas where most employees do not interact with the general public or the end customers.
- ▶ Is money or confidential information being handled by second chance employees?
- ▶ Is there anything to be gained by advertising this aspect of the company?

One approach that makes sense from both a talent-acquisition standpoint and a public relations view is when a second chance hiring initiative is part of a more broadly inclusive program. Cascade Engineering has transformed more than eight hundred lives with its Welfare to Career hiring program. The program includes people with criminal records, and also serves anyone marginalized from the workforce by poverty. In Cascade's highly successful initiative, the use of pipelines from nonprofits and availability of dedicated support services for the employees are essentially the same as in the True Second Chance Model, but the talent pool is even larger, and the public face of the program does not lead with the perceived negatives associated with a criminal record in a worker's background.

Any concerns over public relations negatives should certainly be weighed against public relations positives. In 2019, the prestigious Business Roundtable sought to expand the role of corporations to include the concerns of stakeholders and not just shareholders. The resulting document, "Statement of the Purpose of a Corporation," begins with the sentence, "Americans deserve an economy that allows each person to succeed through hard work and creativity and to lead a life of meaning and dignity."[2] While some have pushed back against any corporate goal that does not focus solely on shareholder value, at a minimum, this statement reflects a public desire for corporations playing a broader role in society. The Deloitte Millennial Survey has consistently shown that this large demographic is interested in both working for and patronizing businesses that provide benefits beyond product or paycheck.[3] Second chance hiring, with its enormous potential to do societal good, obviously feeds this appetite, and can be used as a positive for the brand.

Dave's Killer Bread, a brand with $694 million in sales in 2019, prominently features its second chance hiring on its website and on each package of bread. Nehemiah Manufacturing recently instituted a hang tag on some of its products that proclaims, "Amazing People Made This Product." Opening the folded tag reveals an employee photo and text that includes: "Our mission is simple: Creating jobs for those who need a second chance, whether it's due to a criminal record or barriers that have prevented sustainable employment. We believe in second chances; second chances prove that we can do better after we fall short." At California-based U.S. Rubber Recycling, where two-thirds of the workforce is second chance, CEO Jeff Baldassari created a marketing campaign, "Bounce Back!" Jeff wrote that it "captures who we are—a manufacturer who provides a second chance to employees that give a second life to a discarded product."[4] Baldassari proudly features the story of an employee every Friday on the company's LinkedIn page.

These companies clearly believe that their public acknowledgment of second chance hiring is a positive, not a negative. If your company is a vendor to other companies or governments, a second chance hiring program may offer more than goodwill—it may qualify for vendor pricing or preference advantages.

LLOYD MARTIN: THE CORPORATE EXECUTIVE

There is a reason why most of the businesspeople who have pioneered True Second Chance Models are CEOs and owners of their
companies. Few employees outside the C-suite would be given the
leeway or take the career risks to continue in the trial-and-error
process that has been needed to make second chance hiring a viable business proposition. Lloyd Martin is the exception—an executive whose professional credibility and personal values aligned with
the values of his employer and commanded the respect of its ownership. Leveraging those tools, he applied an engineer's mind and
a compassionate heart to create a second chance hiring program
across five states.

Lloyd is the vice president of manufacturing for CKS Packaging.
The family-owned company (and Lloyd is not a family member)
makes plastic containers in seven states with a large portfolio of
household-name customers. CKS considers itself a "Covenant company," a company that in its founding in 1986 was "dedicated to
God." The headquarters, located in Atlanta, includes what they call
a War Room, dually used for meetings and prayer.

In a company already deeply involved in ministry to the poor
and tithing, Lloyd was in the War Room, praying on how they could
do more. He emerged convinced that CKS could help transform
lives through employing marginalized workers. He shared with me
the story of approaching the company patriarch with his proposal.
Lloyd laid out his idea and how he had come to it through prayer.
The CEO responded, "If God told you to do this, who am I to stand
in the way?"

Starting with five homeless men in Atlanta, Lloyd quickly learned
the need to make accommodations for workers who had very

limited experience of working, or access to the most basic tools of employment. In one of his early learning experiences, he understood the need to abandon rigid HR policies, including the traditional "no show, no call, no job" rule. A solid worker from that first cohort did not show and did not call. Rather than terminate the employee, Lloyd sought him out to learn that the employee was ill. The worker had the good judgment to know not to go to work, but had never been taught to call in, as he reminded Lloyd, "I don't have a phone; I don't have any friends with phones."

Within three years, the program expanded to four states and included more than two hundred hires with a background of criminal records, homelessness, or addiction. True to his engineering roots, Lloyd knows the exact number of second chance hires at any time and can recite the retention and turnover rates for the program at each facility. He seeks continuous improvement in these numbers. Lloyd also looks beyond the numbers and stresses that reentry is not enough. Providing a job and the tools for continued employment may be necessary but is not sufficient. Lloyd argues that, ultimately, second chance hires need reintegration. He defines reintegration as the ability to build a new community based on healthy values and relationships.

Developing a second chance program is hard work, but Lloyd is no stranger to work; when he travels to the company's twenty-two plants, he typically arrives before 4:30 a.m. and stays until 5:00 p.m. so that he can visit with all three shifts. Lest the reader think that Lloyd doesn't know how to kick back and relax, he spends his free time training for Spartan races.

▶ ▶ ▶

Laying Down the Hammer: Accountability

At some point, the internal communication and legal viability groundwork are done. Some leaders may be fortunate to have the executive team and the employee base embrace second chance hiring, but this is probably the exception. Realistically, a leader will reach a level of lukewarm compliance, and maybe even some pockets of passive-aggressive resistance. Particularly in large organizations (the largest firm I've worked for had more than a quarter million employees when I was there), we've all seen workers "slow-walk" or just give lip service to initiatives they oppose. At some point, the leader simply has to make the decision to go forward and require accountability.

Jeff Brown started his successful second chance program with a quota—six hires. This would ultimately grow a hundredfold (literally!) organically, but was still a modest goal for a company with thousands of workers. "If you can't find six qualified hires with records in the city of Philadelphia, the problem is not the applicant pool," Brown reasoned.

The vast majority of second chance employers started with small trials. One chief human resource officer in the hospitality business shared with me that his program started by taking a chance with a single individual and grew to four hundred second chance hires, the founding of a major reentry nonprofit, and successfully petitioning state regulatory bodies to broaden career opportunities for people with records, bringing to life the proverb "From little acorns do mighty oaks grow." His advice: "If they earned the right to a second chance, I think that we in the employment world should give them an opportunity. It has to be one that is very controlled in the beginning so that companies and hiring managers and supervisors gain their confidence in dealing with a group like this. It's not that these people are all that different, it's just that they have very little experience and confidence with them." Of course, it is far better to have a trial with several hires—every manager knows that not every employee will work out, even among hires with pristine credentials.

Beyond quotas, managers and executives have numerous tools to encourage support. Depending on the industry, variable compensation (bonuses) is commonly tied to performance metrics, and some aspect of second chance hiring can certainly be incorporated. Even without a monetary bonus structure, performance reviews and advancement opportunities are powerful incentives in any company. The success of a second chance employee, not merely the fact of hiring, is the corporate goal, so any metric should be well thought out to ensure alignment. As noted in Chapter Four's discussion of potential nonprofit partners, measuring placement and not success can lead to bad hires that can undermine the entire initiative.

Implementation: Legal, Tax, and Talent Pipeline Resources

Among the many collateral consequences associated with a criminal record are outright exclusions from certain regulated industries. However, *DO NOT ASSUME*. In one Midwestern city, I know of a hospital system where the leadership asserted that it was not allowed to hire people with records, while down the road another system has more than a hundred second chance employees. Many executives have risen through the ranks without ever looking into the actual regulations that govern such hiring—misconceptions and outdated information are common. Moreover, even in industries that have legal restrictions, these barriers may only pertain to certain roles, or there may be a process for receiving an exemption.

Besides industry regulations, the legal review should consider other types of restrictions. One company with no automatic disqualifications relocated its manufacturing plant closer to a school, and was then required to institute an employment ban of people on the sex offender list.

An important consideration for companies that send workers to their customer locations is whether those worksites restrict their vendors from using people with records at their sites. This has come up several times with healthcare facilities that have not allowed people with records to move equipment or do electrical work. In the case of healthcare, the Johns Hopkins Health System's second chance hiring program suggests that hospital restrictions are not regulatory but the result of internal rules that may or may not have been well thought out, although some of these restrictions are by law. A friend with a felony conviction serves part-time as the general counsel to a small family manufacturing business. Because the company does some defense-related business, my friend is not allowed in that section of the plant because of his record, despite being an executive. It will not come as a surprise to many readers that not every regulation is consistent or sensible, but accurate knowledge of any governing regulations is a critical starting point.

Beyond any outright restrictions on employment, hiring and screening applicants with criminal records—in other words, the HR process itself—is governed by a body of federal, state, and even local law and regulations. The regulatory interpretation and enforcement of these regulations can also be uneven. Fortunately, this is not particularly burdensome for the second chance employer as this body of law was designed to restrict inappropriate discrimination against people with records, not to punish employers who are open to hiring ex-offenders.

A good starting place for reviewing legal issues associated with the HR process is the excellent digital "toolkit" from the Society of Human Resource Management (SHRM), the premier trade, education, and credentialing organization for human resource professionals. As part of an initiative launched in January 2019, SHRM broke down second chance employment into five broad steps as part of the "Getting Talent Back to Work" Toolkit.[5] This is a great resource for many elements of the second chance hiring process, far beyond just the legal requirements, reaching into corporate culture-building, nonprofit partner directories, onboarding, and mentoring skills. The SHRM toolkit also includes links to another good resource, a video-rich "playbook" for second chance hiring created by Dave's Killer Bread Foundation, the nonprofit arm of a prominent second chance employer.[6] Of course, employers will naturally want to consult their own legal advisors for updated information and local regulations.

In addition to exploring restrictions, companies should also explore the potential financial benefits tied to hiring people with records. The best known of these is the Work Opportunity Tax Credit (WOTC). Although other groups are eligible, within the context of a second chance program, it governs employees who were hired within one year of either a felony conviction or prison release, and delivers a tax credit equal to between 25 percent and 40 percent of qualifying wages. In my experience, small- and medium-sized second chance employers do not rely on this tax credit, finding the administrative process cumbersome. However, many payroll service providers have actively pursued partnering with employers to administer this program on their behalf. Ryan Bergstrom, the chief product officer of Paycor, a payroll processing and HR software company, views the WOTC program not just as a tax benefit, but as a way to "create a more diverse workforce which has been shown time and again to improve business results. Many companies don't utilize the program because of the perceived administrative burden. Human capital management software with WOTC functionality can help lift this burden off of employers, enabling them to capture the financial benefits of the program and invest more in the training and support for the marginalized workers targeted by the WOTC program. It's a win-win."[7] Second chance workers may also be eligible for up to 50 percent subsidies under the Workforce Innovation and Opportunity Act (WIOA) through an on-the-job training (OJT) program administered at the state level through American Job Centers/Workforce Boards. Finally, another resource is the Federal Bonding Program, which offers employers protection of up to $5,000 with no deductible against losses incurred in the first six months of employment.[8] Second chance employers stress that these subsidies should not be the motivation for hiring people with records, but they may be beneficial in defraying some of the associated costs.

Of course, one of the most important parts of implementation is in identifying and building relationships with nonprofit partners. Chapter Four discusses this at length, but it is worth reinforcing that any second chance program can only be as good as its referral sources and its support network. From the standpoint of employee referrals, different businesses find different solutions, but they will generally fit into one of two categories: government entities (prisons, jails, probation/parole offices, courts) and nonprofits (workforce development agencies, reentry nonprofits, halfway houses). For the support of existing second chance hires, the employer will most likely need relationships or at least a referral network that can provide support for housing, transportation, health, and legal/debt issues. While this sounds like a monumental task, in early stages it may be no more than having a name and telephone number at the ready. There is no shortcut to finding the right partners, just persistent exploration and trial-and-error experience.

The Screening Process

The formal screening process begins not with a background check, but with the decision whether to have a section on the application where the applicant discloses any past criminal records, colloquially known as the "Box." There is no requirement that employers include the Box, and increasingly the Box has been banned by governing jurisdictions ("Ban the Box" policies are discussed in greater detail in Chapter Seven). Even in those places where employers are allowed to ask up front about a criminal record, those interested in accessing the broadest talent pool should question whether they want to include the Box on their application. Matt Joyce, partner at Envoy Growth, a consulting firm that specializes in assisting large companies to deploy second chance hiring, makes a compelling case that employers willing to consider people with criminal records should simply exclude the Box voluntarily from their applications. Joyce argues that the very presence of the Box discourages applicants and risks setting up a two-track system for handling applications, with those where the Box is checked automatically disadvantaged.

Even if the Box is retained, employers should be wary of asking for self-disclosure of crimes. Joyce observed, "The box eliminates countless qualified candidates for discrepancies between their responses and the results of the background check. Employers may default to assuming these discrepancies are dishonesty but, given the complexity of the legal system and the resulting data relied upon by background checks, it may easily be the result of misinterpretation, flawed data, and out-of-date information."[9] This may seem incredible to the casual observer, but I know of a professional fired from a firm after four years of productive contribution because he thought a disorderly conduct charge at age eighteen was not on his record, so he had not disclosed it. It had not showed on any previous background checks, but surfaced when he applied for additional licensing to further his career.

A related decision in the screening process concerns how far back any background check goes that you utilize in the probe. Joyce points out that the bulk of recidivism occurs within the first three years after release from prison, so a three-year look-back period is reasonable to assess rehabilitation. Certain background checks are governed by state and federal law, notably the Fair Credit Reporting Act (FCRA), which limits the reporting of civil suits/judgments and arrests without convictions for seven years.

While the FRCA does not limit the reporting period of actual criminal convictions, state law or employer choice may do so. Checkr, a consumer reporting agency that has also championed second chance hiring, provides a partial list of state regulations,[10] as do several other providers. Checkr not only provides background checks but is a second chance employer itself. Daniel Yanisse, CEO and co-founder of Checkr, advises: "Those are the regulatory limits but you should think critically about charges that are most relevant to the role at hand and consider guidelines provided by the Equal Employment Opportunities Commission. For example, does it matter if the candidate has a driving violation if they will never have to drive for the job?" Yanisse further suggests, "It's important to look at your background check provider through a partner lens. In addition to screening new employees, your provider should also offer technology to help you further your diversity and inclusion initiatives by filtering out charges that are irrelevant to the role you're hiring for. This allows you to tap into a wider, more diverse pool of talent and create opportunities for people of all backgrounds—which in turn will breed creativity, innovation, and disruption at your organization."[11]

For industries that have broad statutory disqualifications for people convicted of certain crimes, it may simply be less practical to exclude the Box or to shorten the look-back period of a background check. Even companies that use the Box and self-disclosure can limit unnecessarily narrowing their talent pool by only treating applications differently if a disqualifying offense is self-disclosed, not automatically penalizing a failure to self-disclose a non-disqualifying conviction, and ensuring an even-handed final review process.

Ultimately, the question should boil down to what is effective. Employers can still run background checks (and, from a liability standpoint, they should) at a later point and let applicants respond. Joyce shared the experience of one of his consulting clients. A large corporate client eliminated the Box on the application, limited background checks to shorter look-back periods, and changed the constituency of the review team. Taking these steps reduced the rate of disqualification from 20 percent to 5 percent, and the company's second chance pilot is showing tremendous retention and employee advancement.

Individualized Assessments and the Secondary Review Process

It goes without saying that a hiring manager should have no more knowledge of an applicant's background than any other candidate's health, religion, or other private information. Just as with these other facets of a candidate's life, if hiring managers learn of these, they may not pursue this in interviews, nor can it be a consideration in the hiring decision. Realistically, some applicants may choose to disclose this information, so it is important for managers to feel they have the latitude to pick the best candidate regardless of whether they have a criminal background. The decision about whether a background is a disqualification should be left to a secondary review process, the proper construction of which is an important element of successful second chance programs.

In certain states and for certain employers, a formal background check and review can only take place after a contingent offer of employment has been extended. In others, it may occur earlier in the process. The presence of a criminal record is, at minimum, a complication. For those employers committed to exploring or advancing second chance employment, a further review process is required. Issues surrounding the secondary review are the individualized assessment of each candidate, any automatically disqualifying offenses, and who should participate in this level of review.

As appropriate, the secondary review process should revolve around an individualized assessment. When an arrest or conviction raises a question of whether an applicant should be hired, this is a process that allows for communicating the issue to the applicant, providing an opportunity to respond and clarify, and setting criteria by which to judge the decision. From the employer's standpoint, this is an important opportunity to make sure talent is not overlooked. From the applicant's standpoint, this is not only a chance to correct records with incorrect information, but to provide potentially mitigating circumstances. The US Equal Employment Opportunity Commission (EEOC) offers appropriate examples of appropriate considerations in judging the applicant:

▶ The facts or circumstances surrounding the offense
   or conduct;

▶ The number of offenses for which the individual was convicted;

▶ Older age at the time of conviction, or release from prison;

▶ Evidence that the individual performed the same type of work, post-conviction, with the same or a different employer, with no known incidents of criminal conduct;

▶ The length and consistency of employment history before and after the offense or conduct;

▶ Rehabilitation efforts, for example, education/training;

▶ Employment or character references and any other information regarding fitness for the particular position; and

▶ Whether the individual is bonded under a federal, state, or local bonding program.[12]

Automatically disqualifying offenses can be a particularly important consideration, especially in early stages of second chance hiring. Employers consistently report that maintaining flexibility is important. Even something that required an applicant to register as a sex offender might not be a disqualification; for example, a 2007 Human Rights Watch report noted that at least thirteen states required registration for public urination and twenty-nine states required registration for consensual sex between teenagers. To offer someone a chance to contribute to your company and rebuild his or her life is not to condone the act. Jeff Brown, the CEO of Brown's Super Stores, shared a practical rule of thumb: "Many of these crimes are matters of public record—I want to be able to defend my decisions to a customer, but the number of automatic disqualifications declines the more experience we have."

Brown also provided perspective on crimes of violence: "If you are in the drug trade for any period of time, you are likely to get a crime of violence on your record. People in the trade carry guns to protect their inventory. If a crime happens, even those who did not pull the trigger can be charged with a violent crime even if not specifically engaged in the violent act itself."[13] Each company gets to establish its own criteria.

The "what" of acceptable criteria is one decision, but the "who" is just as important—who decides whether an applicant can be hired is a critical consideration. No matter the composition of this review team, there needs to be accountability to ensure that the answer is not always a rejection. At Cascade Engineering, the review is carried out by a company executive. If delegated to employees below the executive level, a committee approach may help provide balance and lessen the perceived risks to any one employee for making a bad hire. Having a member or members of a review committee from different areas of the company can have value as can having a system where one member advocates for the applicant. The point is not to tip the scales toward an inappropriate hire, but to recognize that there is already inherent bias against hiring someone with a record, and there is a need to develop a system that creates a process grounded in fair consideration and finding the best person for the job.

Onboarding, Coaching, and Support

Supporting sustainable employment is every bit as important as the job itself in second chance hiring. Many hires from the second chance category have limited exposure to the norms of working: attendance, handling criticism, appropriate dress. While a hire does not have to come from a workforce development nonprofit, a successful partnership with such nonprofits creates a baseline of appropriate conduct for second chance employees and also gives them a resource independent of their company for addressing issues. Some employers who meet viable candidates through other channels will insist that prospective applicants start by meeting or enrolling with their nonprofit partners.

The specific internal tools for supporting second chance hires vary by company size and experience. Often, companies that have come to second chance hiring had already been hiring workers from more challenged backgrounds and established support mechanisms. When Nehemiah Manufacturing CEO Dan Meyer told me, "I don't have HR people. I have social workers," I thought he was speaking figuratively, but his HR team actually were social workers. "Life coaches" and "chance coaches" have become an increasingly common presence in companies and are a natural point of contact for second chance (and other) hires.

For the many companies that do not have social workers/life coaches on staff, external support resources become key. Even companies with deep internal resources lean heavily on external partners. Commonly, these are nonprofits that can assist with housing, food security, financial assistance (commonly credit counseling), and education. Skender, the Chicago home builder and second chance employer, was struggling with a second chance hire who had difficulty accepting criticism. The company resolved this successfully by partnering with the employee's union, which sent a seasoned union brother to work with the employee. Atlanta's CKS Packaging worked with the Atlanta Transit Authority to change a bus route to better accommodate their second chance hires' needs. Most second chance employers find there are an abundance of potential partners to help support their employees.

Several highly advanced second chance employers show what those partnerships and support services look like to their second chance hires. Nehemiah Manufacturing works with twenty-five to thirty different nonprofits, with different levels of engagement with their 180 employees, and spends roughly $300,000 a year in donations. Wellness and health programs include Alcoholics Anonymous programs within their facility, given how alcohol and drug addiction are common drivers of criminal records. CEO Dan Meyer stresses, "It's important to have programs that prevent people from slipping and falling."[14] All their employees can take advantage of a gym on-site, but when management observed that many employees felt uncomfortable exercising around their peers, the company introduced a $500 per year benefit for a personal trainer or going to a gym of the employee's choice. Other partnerships include housing, medical services, transportation, and education.

Education is an important element of the employee support programming. CEO Ray Dalton of reLink Medical makes a persuasive business case: "Build people who have a higher value of themselves and they will turn out a better product."[15] His company offers a Life Center encompassing much of this programming. Resources include online education programs paid for by the company and a computer lab for employee use. Those wishing to advance their careers at reLink Medical are expected to complete five hours a month of online education—it is not required that it be relevant to the job.

Dalton's Life Center programming encompasses areas of education far outside traditional academic or vocational skills. He partners with Brooks Brothers to discuss appropriate dress. A local restaurant teaches restaurant etiquette.

This could be mistaken for a patronizing approach, but Dalton, like other second chance leaders, understands that many basic skills that may be taken for granted by those with more privileged upbringings can be intimidating roadblocks for people with different backgrounds. The business community is long accustomed to the concept of "gap analysis," identifying and addressing roadblocks to optimal performance. Second chance employees can come with significant gaps, but when these are addressed through empathy and education, they perform.

A critical component of employee support is teaching personal financial management skills. Again, many of the challenges faced by people with records are really the challenges of abject poverty, which are further complicated by a criminal record. Many of the poor go unbanked. According to the 2017 FDIC National Survey of Unbanked and Underbanked Households (conducted biennially), 6.5 percent of American households have no bank account. This number includes many with felony convictions, a group that historically many banks have restricted from opening accounts. An additional 18.7 percent are "underbanked," having a bank account but also relying on the costly alternatives used by the unbanked: check cashing services, payday lenders, pawnshop and auto title loans, and so on. For his hundreds of second chance employees, CEO Jeff Brown stresses that it is critical that everyone have a bank account and eliminate dependence on payday lenders. Brown identifies opening a bank account as the start of financial responsibility.

As part of the financial education process, some employers have arrangements with local banks and credit unions that will open accounts for their second chance hires. Ray Dalton uses one such arrangement to drive financial responsibility even further. In addition to providing a financial education program, the company cosigns a $500 debit card and requires employees to elect direct deposit into an affiliated bank account. Employees agree that the bank will notify the company of any overdraft, and employees face consequences for financial mismanagement. For example, a third overdraft is grounds for termination. Dalton's structure and discipline become the building blocks for his employees' good financial habits and establishment of good credit history.

Second chance employers tend to have strong cultures of coaching and mentorship. It is not uncommon for established second chance hires to play a role in helping newer hires succeed. There is a challenge in that some people with records have not had much experience in being on the receiving end of constructive criticism. One of the important skills that workforce development agencies can impart is the ability to accept criticism in the spirit of developmental coaching, rather than as an affront. Supervisors and managers who understand this background can be more effective, using thoughtful language and confirming that any coaching is to help, not to hurt. Similarly, many people with these backgrounds are unaccustomed to recognition. Reformer John Koufos advises: "Say thank you as often as possible. Returning citizens are accustomed to being told why the world hates them and/or being disrespected. You may be the first person in their lives to ever say thank you."[16]

Quantum Leap Second Chance Hiring: Going to the Next Level

Many of the firms I've researched embrace the continuous expansion and improvement of their second chance hiring programs. There's something engaging about watching your teammates contribute to your company while also building lives beyond their imagining for themselves and their families. As a general rule, second chance employers tend to add more and more services for their employees, broadening the scope of acceptable backgrounds and constantly challenging their program to innovate further.

The experienced second chance employer, one who has set up internal support resources, can become less reliant on nonprofits that do workforce preparation and preliminary vetting. Several specific electronic "job boards" are available for employers looking to target the community of people with records, including 70Million-Jobs.com and Honestjobs.co. Both were founded by formerly incarcerated entrepreneurs.

Another path for hiring is temp agencies. The traditional challenge with temp-to-hire versus direct hiring is the risk that your temp worker is "snatched away" by another employer willing to offer a permanent position. People with criminal records are rarely in such demand, so employers can reap the benefit of temp-to-hire, taking advantage of the opportunity to test potential employees.

Cooperative arrangements with prisons and halfway houses also offer a productive path. The Dalton Foundation of Ohio recently structured a model of a prison-to-job pipeline, the Workforce Development Collaborative:

In this program, minimum security inmates from the Grafton Reintegration Center, who are 6 months or less from their scheduled release dates, are carefully screened through [a] rigorous interview process for placement in an externship at the reLink Medical warehouse. Successful candidates will have graduated from one of [nonprofit] True Freedom's intensive programs, completed a pre-release vocational training program, and will have been approved for community approved statuses by the Ohio Department of Rehabilitation and Corrections (ODRC).[17]

Coordinating government agencies, a faith-based nonprofit, and an informed employer create what the Dalton Foundation refers to as "Holistic Second Chance Employment," but the reader will readily recognize it as a variation of the True Second Chance Model identified in this book.

Finally, I would be remiss if I did not mention the incredible business and community leadership shown by second chance pioneers. Many of them have gone on to create nonprofits and other civic initiatives to help more businesses develop second chance hiring. The Dalton Foundation mentioned here is but one of several with which I'm familiar. Dan Meyer's Beacon of Hope Business Alliance, the numerous civic initiatives built by Mark Peters and Fred Keller, and Jeff Brown's Uplift Solutions all bear witness to the visionary thinking of these leaders. These businesses are giving away their competitive advantage in accessing this labor pool, and they not only do this voluntarily, they do so at considerable personal commitment of time and money. This is truly admirable and deserving of our support and recognition.

Zen Master Level Second Chance Hiring

If you were a Zen master, how would you do second chance hiring? We already know the answer to that because of Greyston Bakery in Yonkers, New York. Recently retired Greyston CEO Mike Brady described open hiring in practical terms in an interview with MIT's Sloan School of Management: "You walk through the door, put your name on a list, [and] when we have another job available we take the next name off the list [with] no questions asked. No background checks, no reference checks, no interviews."[18]

Bernie Glassman pioneered "open hiring" at Greyston Bakery. Trained as an engineer and ultimately earning a doctorate in applied mathematics from UCLA, Glassman followed a different path, becoming a Zen Buddhist roshi (roughly translated, "master"). In 1982, Glassman opened the Greyston Bakery in Yonkers as a way to employ his Zen students, but over time began to expand, offering jobs to the homeless in the neighborhood. The company grew, becoming a supplier of brownies to Ben & Jerry's ice cream and then Whole Foods Market. It is a Certified B Corp, setting an example of profitable open hiring through the nonprofit Greyston Center for Open Hiring. Seventy of the bakery's one hundred employees came through open hiring.

Joe Kenner, current CEO, observes that, just like second chance hiring, this is a business proposition with benefits of low turnover and high engagement, but requiring an investment in wraparound services. The open hiring variation has the added benefit of low recruiting costs and a broader applicant pool.

Retailer The Body Shop initiated a trial of open hiring in a North Carolina distribution center, with an applicant screen of only three questions:

1. Are you authorized to work in the United States?
2. Can you stand for up to eight hours?
3. Can you lift more than fifty pounds?

The results of lower turnover have been so good that the chain is looking to expand open hiring to their retail stores.

Greyston and the Start Foundation have begun promoting open hiring in the Netherlands, where it has been adopted by a handful of firms. The website of one Dutch company, Chain Logistics, describes the process to potential applicants:

You cannot apply to us with a letter. We do not need your CV. We don't find your past, where you come from, what kind of faith you have, how old you are, how many diplomas you have. You decide whether you are suitable for the vacancy!

The only condition we set is that you come to us. That is the sign for us that you want the job. When you visit us, we will receive you with a cup of coffee or tea. We tell you something about Chain Logistics and about the job. If that feels right to you, put your name on a list. If a vacancy becomes available, you will be the next to get the job. It's that simple![19]

I do not know the true viability of this model of hiring. I certainly suspect it is better suited for some industries than others. Food manufacturing and preparation have generally been "felon-friendly," and perhaps it is no coincidence that two of the nation's most prominent second chance employers are bakers: Greyston and Dave's Killer Bread. But open hiring works for Greyston and appears to be working for The Body Shop, and ultimately offers a very hopeful message to the readers of this book who aspire to employ those in need of a second chance. If open hiring can work, and we choose to be selective in our hiring through the processes of the True Second Chance Model, how can we fail to succeed?

CASE STUDY—
JBM PACKAGING

I don't know where we'd be today
without our fair chance hires.
—MARCUS SHEANSHANG, *CEO*

Chapter Four outlines the successful model, Chapter Five provides a road map for implementation, and in this chapter, you will see how this actually worked for one successful Ohio manufacturing company. Using the categories of implementation discussed in the preceding pages, this chapter will chronicle the journey taken by this second-generation, family-owned manufacturing business as it introduced second chance hires.

As of June 2020, in less than four years since their first hire with a criminal record, 31 of JBM's 150 current employees came through their second chance hiring initiative. JBM's second chance (in their parlance, "fair chance") hiring program ended up not only bolstering its workforce but also transforming the company in profoundly positive ways.

Background

The JBM Envelope Company was founded in 1985 by Greg Sheanshang. A quintessential family-owned company, the initials in the company title are derived from the names of Sheanshang's children: Jennifer, Bridget, and Marcus. Such family businesses make up the backbone of the American economy, although their contributions are often overlooked in a world where the companies that are publicly traded on the New York Stock Exchange or NASDAQ capture all the headlines in the business press.

According to studies cited by the Conway Center for Family Business, family enterprises account for 64 percent of US GDP and 78 percent of job creation. In the goods-producing economy, it often takes more than one generation to build the sort of resources required to scale capital-intensive manufacturing, and these companies provide vital links in the supply chain. These are companies that have survived numerous recessions, credit crises, and displacement by new technologies and consumer preferences. The Conway Center and similar organizations note the agility and entrepreneurship found in family-owned businesses. At JBM, this spirit of innovation manifested in the company's implementation of second chance hiring.

I have had the great fortune of meeting many pioneers in the creation of second chance hiring programs. All of them are worthy of case studies in their own right, and one, Nehemiah Manufacturing, has already been published as a case study by Harvard Business School,[1] but JBM stuck out. Many businesses can relate to JBM's challenges and culture and be better equipped to evaluate their own potential to develop a talent pipeline of people with criminal records. My selection is also a recognition of the openness and generosity with which its CEO, Marcus Sheanshang, and his team have been willing to share setbacks, mistakes, and, ultimately, the company's triumphs.

Some leaders have built companies from the ground up as second chance employers, or came themselves from a family with justice-involvement, or operated a B Corp or other social enterprise with a deep desire to address social ills. That is not the case with JBM. By all appearances, Marcus Sheanshang came to second chance hiring as an ordinary businessman with an ordinary business problem. But with Sheanshang's leadership, the way this initiative changed the company and the lives of its employees was extraordinary.

The Leader's Role: Building the Vision

After Marcus Sheanshang purchased his father's company, the executive team created a straightforward mission statement: "Dominate targeted small, open-end envelope markets." Such envelopes had been the company's core business and the legacy inherited along with the name, JBM Envelope Company. Open-end envelopes have numerous applications and opportunities for sales growth: seed packets, coin envelopes for banks, room key card holders for hotels, and so on. But to fulfill the mission of dominating that market required more workers. Like many companies in the 2014–2019 period, JBM's growth was severely retarded by its lack of ability to attract a quality workforce.

JBM's challenges in attracting workers were common among American businesses. During this period, job openings exceeded the number of job-seekers in the US economy to a degree never before recorded. The goods-producing economy was particularly short-handed. Manufacturing careers were often discouraged by parents in a culture that put excessive emphasis on college degrees and the service economy. Like almost all manufacturers whose employees work with machinery, drug testing is required to ensure workplace safety. For most of the past decade, employers have raised the alarm about how the opioid epidemic was severely restricting the qualified labor pool, and this was an even larger challenge in JBM's backyard. Ohio has ranked second only to West Virginia in opioid overdose death rates.[2]

On top of these challenges was JBM's location. Nearly thirty miles outside the city center of Cincinnati, Lebanon is a town of twenty thousand people, settled in the late eighteenth century and once known for a nearby Shaker settlement. It is the Warren County seat, the county's only train service is a scenic train ride, and the only public bus service runs from Cincinnati to the Kings Island amusement park. While Cincinnati and its large labor force were not far away, the distance was insurmountable for workers without a car.

JBM's Executive Team identified the lack of labor as the company's biggest "gap," and the company tried to develop different pipelines for workers. Tour after tour of local high school students attracted no workers. Attempts to lure older workers were unproductive. The company was left with temp-to-hire labor, an expensive option that produced spotty results at best.

In 2016, Sheanshang was introduced to the concept of second chance hiring through his church, Crossroads. Crossroads is a multisite interdenominational church with locations in Ohio and Kentucky. One of the fastest growing churches in America, on any given weekend more than 34,000 people attend services and 6,000 participate each week over the internet. The church is no stranger to providing hope and opportunity to the poor and marginalized; it built and operates Citylink, a 76,000-square-foot facility that houses multiple nonprofits that offer holistic and coordinated support, with critical staffing filled by ten teams of Crossroads volunteers.

Early on, Sheanshang started discussing the concept of second chance hiring with his Executive Team. At this time, Dan Puthoff, JBM's COO, was introduced to Dan Meyer of Nehemiah Manufacturing, the founder of Beacon of Hope Business Alliance, the nonprofit that supports and promotes other businesses following Nehemiah's path in second chance hiring. Through Crossroads, Sheanshang met officials of the Ohio Department of Rehabilitation and Correction (ODRC). The seed was planted. Perhaps the workforce gap could be filled with people coming from prison and others with a criminal record. This was a potential solution to a business problem. At least here was a workforce that nobody else wanted.

Communication and Overcoming Objections

JBM structures its management team into two groups, the Executive Team and the Leadership Team. Leadership Team members are generally supervisors, including the shift supervisors typically responsible for twenty-five to thirty team members. The company operates around the clock, requiring communications to three separate shifts.

Sheanshang began discussing the concept with his Executive Team. There was little enthusiasm and plenty of outright skepticism. Christine Stroup, who oversaw HR, observed that among people in her position, "For years it has been ingrained in folks, 'don't go there.'"[3] Outside the office, even Sheanshang's father, the company founder, thought the idea was crazy.

The objections were focused largely on the unknown—who were these people? To the degree objections could be categorized, they boiled down to safety and performance.

An early ally in introducing second chance hiring was Ashley Caudill, a human resources supervisor with a broad background in employee relations and HR policy drafting. Caudill joined JBM in 2016 with an interest in recruiting, hoping that proactively seeking new employees would prove more effective than temp-to-hire.

Caudill had to be won over herself. She personally had no familiarity with people with records, and admitted, "At first I wasn't sure." Over time, she learned, "when it works, it works!"

Caudill became a point person for employees concerned with JBM's new fair chance initiative. Some of the most doubtful employees were JBM's most tenured team members, longtime strong contributors to the company's success, and their opposition represented a real business risk. Caudill took these skeptics as a professional and personal challenge. If she could not completely win them over to hire people with records, she could at least work to reduce the negativity and urge them not to prejudge the program or the people. Many of these objections centered on concerns over the quality of second chance hires. Caudill's approach was to humanize those with records. In her conversations with concerned employees, she asked them to recall mistakes they had made in their own lives. If they were not defined by their worst days, others should not be defined by theirs.

Sheanshang also personalized his response to objections. To the degree safety concerns surfaced, he reminded his colleagues that he expected his young children would one day work at the family company, and he would never compromise the safety of his son and daughter's future workplace. Indeed, on my visit to the company in

June 2020, both his children, then teens, were working on the factory floor.

JBM's Executive Team also examined the challenge of overcoming objections related to the quality of workers with criminal records. They had been calling their initiative a "second chance" program, but felt it was too easy to conflate second chance with second rate. For JBM, this program would become and be maintained as their Fair Chance Program. Who could object to "fair"? In this chapter, *second chance* and *fair chance* are used interchangeably.

Repetition of a consistent message signified management's commitment to the initiative. As the program progressed, Sheanshang made sure the message was reinforced with the Leadership Team and monthly company meetings with all three shifts.

One component of JBM's communication strategy was providing education to the Executive and Leadership Teams, not only in the earliest stages, but even after their first fair chance hires. The company sent the director of marketing and the vice president of sales/ marketing to Pickaway Correctional Institution, a visit that proved transformational in getting them on board with the initiative. Members of the Executive Team increasingly traveled to several prisons as part of their education process, which also helped in communicating the strategy to the broader company. COO Puthoff explained, "The early visits were important as they gave us, as leaders, credibility when we were discussing the program internally. We felt comfortable enough to enter the walls of prison and be with the prisoners in close quarters—we didn't believe we were compromising safety at JBM as we looked to start hiring more reformed citizens."[4]

A critical turning point in winning over the teams were separate visits to Cincinnati's Nehemiah Manufacturing and its long established second chance hiring. Puthoff took two other executives to visit Nehemiah and described the impact:

> In the first month of speaking about this prior to my visit to Nehe-
> miah, I viewed it as a viable strategy to build production capacity.
> After that visit to Nehemiah, I viewed it as that, in addition to pro-
> viding JBM and me personally, the ability to play a transformational
> role in the lives of our team members in a more profound way than
> we had in the past. Before leaving Nehemiah that day, I told Dan
> Meyer how inspirational the visit was and that I would love to see
> JBM become the "Nehemiah of Warren County." At this point, I was
> all in.[5]

Nehemiah's success is so self-evident and its management's enthusiasm so infectious that it is hard to walk away without believing in
the potential of a second chance workforce. JBM continues to use
visits to Nehemiah as a tool to educate new and aspiring managers on
the potential of their Fair Chance Program.

As the company explored potential partners, Executive Team
members became increasingly convinced of the potential for their
Fair Chance Program. The Executive Team would speak with one
voice.

Laying Down the Hammer: Accountability

Toward the end of the communication phase, a critical point was
reached. Sheanshang and the Executive Team had stated their case.
The communication was consistent and the Executive Team was
united. Not every employee was won over, but there was no more to
say; only actual success could change some minds.

The company offers employees a conduit for anonymous questions or comments through an "Ask JBM" box and surveys, and management would provide responses. One unsigned comment stuck out
and is still remembered by the Executive Team: "You should stop the
Fair Chance Program." Sheanshang used his public response to this
comment as the point to draw the line:

> This is the company we are today and the company we will be tomor-
> row. If you can't align yourself with that, this might not be the com-
> pany for you.

By that time in the process, the Executive Team was on board.
There were no quotas. No financial incentives other than the clear
understanding that growing the workforce was the key to their mutual success.

Implementation:
Legal, Tax, and Talent Pipeline Resources

Sheanshang and his Executive Team actively discussed the legal issues
surrounding hiring people with criminal records. Chief among their
concerns was the issue of "negligent hiring liability," the risk that the
company could be sued if there were an incident involving a hire with
a criminal record. In the end, JBM's Executive Team decided that
with an appropriate due-diligence process in talent acquisition, negligent hiring liability was an acceptable business risk. This is not to
say that legal advisor input and liability concerns did not have an
impact. The company had been considering buying a small fleet of
cars for the use of their fair chance hires who did not have their own
transportation. As Sheanshang explained with a laugh, "Our lawyers

convinced us that, from a liability standpoint, this was a bad idea, a very, very bad idea!"

JBM also examined available subsidies for hiring formerly incarcerated workers, but Sheanshang was adamant that this take a back seat to finding the right person for the job. Over time, the company relied on its payroll service provider to process federal tax incentives, including the Work Opportunity Tax Credit (WOTC). While it experimented with state-funded training incentives, the administration of the claims process ultimately proved too burdensome.

In building a talent pipeline, JBM went down unproductive paths at first. Workforce and reentry nonprofits in the area just didn't seem to identify viable candidates, people both ready and interested. Fairly quickly, JBM identified prisons as a more viable source of talent. Even here, early efforts were not promising. Their first attempt at hiring from correctional facilities started with attending "resource fairs" within prisons. These scheduled events offer prison residents the chance to meet with prospective employers and reentry resources. There was little pre-vetting of whom they might meet, and sometimes inmates would attend just to have something to do.

JBM's first fair chance hire came in October 2016, a referral from an employment specialist with the Warren County court system, with whom the company had established a relationship just the month before. JBM was now a second chance employer, but had not yet established a consistent pipeline and process.

The company continued to explore relationships with correctional facilities. The ODRC, the state prison authority, had already created an Office of Enterprise Development (OED) led by Will Eleby to facilitate partnerships and training programs with private sector employers. The OED served as the gatekeeper to businesses that wanted access to prisoners. In December 2016, JBM formally presented its vision to the OED, and the company's application to start working with inmates for post-release employment was approved unanimously. Sheanshang has been consistent in his praise of Eleby and the OED, but notes there can be challenges in working with government structures. "They were very honest. They told us, 'We're the state, it's going to take a while.'" The ODRC and its OED very much value JBM as well—the company appears on the OED website as a successful example of partnership and includes a link to a video produced by the ODRC about the partnership.

JBM found that working with individual correctional facilities met with less consistent success and varying degrees of receptivity. Sheanshang explained: "The way we looked at it when we started was we viewed this as a sales project . . . we're selling to the prison . . . we're selling to the warden . . . some of the prisons say they are interested but then don't return phone calls or emails. We found that some prisons worked, but others weren't responsive and didn't."[6] Even as the program has progressed, JBM values and reinforces the relationship with its talent sources.

Ashley Caudill explained: "I have worked really hard to build relationships with prison staff: case managers, unit leaders, wardens, and others." JBM uses a document found in Appendix B to clarify expectations with prisons and halfway houses prior to recruiting visits. With promising applicants, JBM forges a partnership with the prison's assigned case manager to coordinate the reentry process, including housing and transportation.

Eventually, through outreach and trial and error, JBM focused on two facilities, the Dayton Correctional Institute (a women's prison with a reintegration unit that already did a high degree of prescreening and vetting), thirty miles and forty-five minutes away, and Pickaway Correctional Institution, seventy miles away and a one-hour straight shot north on Interstate 71. Since 2018, JBM went farther afield, including candidates from the Ohio Reformatory for Women, eighty miles away, as well as the London Correctional Institution, sixty-five miles away. Given the distance of the facilities from the plant, one of the very real constraints on the supply of candidates is geography—the willingness of prison residents to resettle within commuting distance of the JBM plant.

More recently, the company expanded its talent pipeline to include halfway houses, supervised housing facilities for people exiting prison. JBM has found this a particularly productive pipeline, finding that the residents are simply further along in the reentry process. The first weeks outside of prison can be overwhelming, with time and energy drained by the uncertainties and challenges of stabilizing housing, getting identification, phones, reconnecting with family . . . all good and necessary, but often a period too distracting to launch a stable career. Those in the halfway facilities are already past some of this transition and ready to focus.

The company is building pipelines from both men's and women's facilities, both of which have provided successful hires, even in the traditionally male-dominated world of manufacturing. On a visit to JBM, I met with a recent second chance hire who had been recruited from a halfway house. Although she was able to leave the facility and return home, she still wore an ankle monitor. She will be JBM's first woman to qualify for a skilled machine maintenance role, a position that industry-wide is nearly exclusively filled by men.

As JBM's reputation as a second chance employer grows, other referral sources are surfacing. Several parole officers have made referrals. The company continues to experiment, placing ads on job boards that target people with records. At present, prisons and halfway houses have been the most productive talent pipelines and remain the focus of JBM's talent acquisition efforts.

JBM was fortunate to have early successes as it hired from prisons. The first came from Pickaway in October 2017. He exited the prison gates at 10:00 a.m. and was driven directly to JBM. His potential was spotted by Marty Cozzi, then JBM's director of operations, who became a mentor to the first hire. Cozzi personally took the new team member to shop for clothes and then got him settled in a halfway house, while others arranged for transportation and housing. That first direct-from-prison hire is still with JBM, a praised and valued team member who has won company awards and is soon going to visit his old prison, not as a resident, but as a trainer for JBM. The company's second direct-from-prison hire, a woman from Dayton Correctional Institution, was also a success and a winner of the company's "Team Member of the Month" award until eventually leaving to raise a family.

As the number of fair chance hires grew, JBM's executives assessed the performance of their hires and the effectiveness of the program. Christine Stroup, vice president of human resources when the program was implemented, has tracked retention, a key measure of success: "Over six to twelve months, it became obvious that this was the best route to get people in and retain them."

Sheanshang made clear that, in the end, the Fair Chance Program participants get no special preference, and it is all about getting the people "who can live our values and make JBM better," not which pipeline brings them to the company. This is business, not charity, and the business case remains strong. He observes that the tight labor market was the catalyst for their second chance hiring, and interest from other companies for this was high for the same reason: "Interest in fair chance hiring might change with 20 percent unemployment. It's not going to change for us."

The Screening Process

In general, JBM focuses on limiting second chance hires only to those convicted of certain lower level crimes, believing this is most consistent with its commitment to making employees feel comfortable and safe. The company has certain nonnegotiable automatic disqualifications for employment: crimes against children, women, or sexual crimes. They will consider someone with violent crime convictions but give those candidates particularly rigorous scrutiny.

Since JBM's Fair Chance Program is working with prisons and halfway houses, the company obviously knows that these candidates already have a record. Nonetheless, JBM hiring managers learned to still get background checks. They learned through experience that not every candidate fully discloses the full record of convictions and circumstances. Although the credit reporting service provides a complete history, JBM places little weight on items that go back further than seven years. For candidates in prison, the background checks are conducted prior to their release date to ensure that successful applicants can start working and rebuilding their lives without unnecessary delay.

The screening process includes tests related to manufacturing careers, the Weisen Test of Mechanical Aptitude, and the Standard Timing Model. The Weisen test is a written exam that assesses the ability to learn to use and maintain mechanical equipment. The Standard Timing Model is a hands-on test with varying degrees of difficulty and assessment that involves physically manipulating the "machine" within the kit. In the words of its vendor, Scientific Management Techniques, Inc., the model is a broad assessment of "mechanical troubleshooting ability." The Standard Timing Model can be used to test existing skill levels of trained personnel. In the typical case of JBM's in-prison candidates, it tests the aptitude for learning among those who have not yet been trained. These are administered by JBM personnel in the prison or halfway house as part of the hiring process.

Recruiting is intertwined with the screening process for JBM. At prisons, this typically occurs quarterly, while visits to halfway houses are monthly. Allison Rambo, the company's change coach, and Ashley Caudill take the lead roles in this recruiting. In prisons, case managers are responsible for identifying viable candidates, while halfway houses will often start with open information sessions that look similar to corporate recruiting on college campus. Every firm that visits is open to second chance hiring, but JBM attracts more candidates (and ultimately finds good fits) by highlighting the highly valued and robust support network it offers its employees. The group presentation is followed by what Allison referred to as "speed interviews," jokingly drawing the parallel to speed dating.

The primary screening tool used in JBM's Fair Chance Program is a questionnaire developed by Rambo. The full document is available in Appendix A, but a sampling of the questions provides a sense of the critical information. "What have you learned about yourself while being incarcerated?" "What are your triggers? How do you cope with triggers?" "How will you live differently?"

Rambo observed: "You can tell who is going to fit the culture and who is not. . . . You need to see that they have self-realization about what got them there, see if they are committed to improving."

Screening at JBM for all employees includes drug testing typical for manufacturing: preemployment, upon reasonable suspicion, and post-accident. For people whose lives had been complicated by addiction, JBM may require hires to accept unannounced, random drug testing.

Individualized Assessments and the Secondary Review Process

JBM does not have a formally structured individualized assessment, although its experience with candidates has led to essentially the same criteria as the Equal Employment Opportunity Commission (EEOC) recommended guidelines. There is no stigma to overcome, just a business decision and a culture that is already looking for a reason to hire someone with a record, not a reason to exclude them.

A critical part of the JBM review process for its Fair Chance Program is the composition of the review committee. It continues to have five members, a balance of HR concerns, business needs, and social service expertise: the director of human capital and culture, the HR recruiter, the company's change coach, the director of operations, and the COO. All are supporters of the Fair Chance Program and approach the review process with the desire to hire, not to discard applicants.

Onboarding, Coaching, and Support

Even before the launch of its Fair Chance Program, JBM's Executive Team observed that, as the labor market tightened, some of its new hires came without all the traditional life skills found in older generations of workers. To address this gap, the company went through several iterations of a life or change coach, starting with part-time support. In 2019, Allison Rambo joined the team as change coach and has become the point person for the suite of support services offered for all employees, not just fair chance hires. Fair chance hires are required to meet with Rambo, and she plays a critical role in the onboarding of employees coming from prison and halfway houses. Both she and Ashley Caudill have been de facto case managers to their employees, identifying ways that the company can assist their team members beyond the workplace.

Although not generally considered a "best practice," JBM is willing to let shift supervisors know if their team members came through the Fair Chance Program. In the early days of the program, this was not the case, and Sheanshang regretted the unnecessary tensions created with that leadership team. He observes, "It takes thirty seconds on the internet for people to find out." Even without a proactive search, team members assume that their colleagues who rely on a shared transportation van have been recently incarcerated, typically an accurate assumption.

Onboarding is a critical time, particularly for JBM's employees just coming from prison, and essentially becomes an extension of prison exit planning. Ashley Caudill outlined her role when a person leaves prison:

> How I help with exit planning is to make sure I speak with them prior to release—over the phone or in person, to make sure they're comfortable with new hire items such as their birth certificate, ID, social security card, transportation, etc. I like to make sure they know I am their touch point upon release to help with a smooth transition. I

always provide my cell phone number to call upon release and/or call prior to release (collect from prison) if we cannot connect via their case manager.[7]

Allison Rambo would take on other elements of the transition to working life outside bars. She developed a framework for change coaching, the Fair Chance Better Lives Plan (see Appendix C for plan documents). Second chance hires are required to sign and adhere to a six-month training commitment and meet weekly with Rambo. The conversations are held in confidence. This is also an opportunity for Rambo to identify opportunities to bring in the outside support partnerships as needed.

Even before Rambo's arrival, JBM had realized it needed to line up support for fair chance hires. At first, such support was done on an ad hoc basis. Over time, the company was able to identify partners. Nonprofit Beacon of Hope provided a van service for employees from Cincinnati. The service is free for the first two weeks (until the first paycheck), then employees pay $5 each way for the transportation and JBM subsidizes the additional cost. Some of the halfway houses also provide transportation. More recently, the company has partnered with the nonprofit Wheels program. This charity provides free cars for those in need. While these cars are safe, they generally are older with a limited expected life, so JBM encourages its employees to set up a "trade-up" fund that the company matches, enabling their employees to buy decent, long-lasting vehicles within a year.

Other nonprofit partners included the New Life Furniture Bank to help with furnishing living spaces. The company enlisted help to support clothing and housing needs. Sharefax Credit Union made second chance accounts and a credit repair program available; team members who had not yet opened accounts received their pay on payroll cards (loaded debit cards) to avoid check-cashing fees. Rambo created a curriculum of life skills classes, often in conjunction with outside partners, called Cultivate Classes, teaching everything from parenting skills to budgeting. Wellness is provided through YMCA/ YWCA memberships or subsidies for those who wish to join health clubs. Sheanshang summed up the investment in education and non-profit partnerships: "We probably spend a couple hundred thousand dollars a year on this program and it is worth every penny of it." He advises prospective second chance employers, "You need to be ready to spend some money."

JBM has enlisted the help of parole officers in sustaining the em-ployment of the fair chance hires. As with nonprofits, not every part-nership is successful, but the successful ones have become deep relationships and even referral sources. The company allows parole officers to meet with employees privately on-site, a convenience for both. "I'm not going to say it's all been good, but we have three or four different parole officers who have been fantastic. . . . We've had some problems they've helped us navigate. . . . It's been about 75 percent good/25 percent bad," in Sheanshang's assessment.

Members of JBM's Executive Team often take a particular respon-sibility for mentoring the second chance hires. Ashley Caudill ex-plained, "We like to stake our claim on people." At the supervisory level, JBM encourages understanding and empathy. After fair chance hiring had already begun, the company's life coach at the time deliv-ered an education session to the leadership group about addiction and other issues that may have been significant challenges in the lives of the team members they supervise. Caudill observed that a little genuine interest in their fair chance hires can go a long way, recount-ing how she checked in with a second chance hire who had been having difficulties. Before answering, the employee exclaimed with surprise, "I've never had anyone ask me, 'Are you okay?'"

Sheanshang is also working to build a culture of mentoring within his fair chance cohort. At his ninety-day review with each employee, he encourages second chance hires to help coach the newer second chance employees. "I think we are going to reach a tipping point when our [second chance] population is about 25 percent or so. . . . We're hitting more and more people who want to be here for the program." Mentoring among returning citizens is not exclusively within the company. As JBM's fair chance hires start to move into supervisory roles, Dan Puthoff is facilitating relationships with Nehemiah Manufacturing's formerly incarcerated supervisors and managers.

JBM's Fair Chance Program has experienced its share of unsuccessful hires, particularly in the earlier stages. One hire "got in the face" of a supervisor (i.e., no physical altercation, but an inappropriate response to direction and criticism). The most common failures were employees who slid back into drug addiction, faced transportation issues, or simply weren't ready for employment. Sheanshang also admits that in the early stages, "We were not fully prepared."

Addressing underperforming employees is always a challenge, but this was particularly complex for JBM initially. The company recognized that accommodations were needed for its second chance hires, but not where to draw the line. Sheanshang admitted: "We led too much with the heart, but have learned that we can only help those who are ready. . . . We still struggle with that. It's a fine line."

Allison Rambo added, "This work is about having a whole lot of compassion and empathy, but having an insane amount of boundaries."

Several members of the Executive Team shared their rule of thumb: "If we have to work harder to keep you employed than you do, it is not going to work."

Quantum Leap Second Chance Hiring: Going to the Next Level

The successes of the Fair Chance Program bred even more innovation. If JBM had stopped at establishing a talent acquisition pipeline with a number of prisons and supplemented that with solid support services, it would have been a great, solid example of a successful practitioner of the True Second Chance Model. But Sheanshang and the company took it further.

Pickaway Correctional Institution (PCI) had been one of several referral sources to JBM, but PCI had something special—a print shop. On the surface, the print shop had the attributes of "prison labor" that are abhorrent to prison reformers—low-paid work whose output is purchased by state agencies. But the printing trade is a skill, and PCI also offered work experience in other industries as well as certificate programs within the prison administered by Sinclair Community College. Far from being a nightmare version of a Victorian workhouse, PCI had strong progressive elements, like a reading room that allowed incarcerated parents to have a comfortable and welcoming space to read to their children. It was also home to OASIS Therapeutic Community, an addiction treatment program, created jointly by the prison, the ODRC, and the state's Department of Mental Health and Addiction. The OASIS initiative, like other therapeutic communities, has shown success in breaking the addiction-driven cycle of reincarceration.

JBM had already had a very positive experience with hiring a resident of PCI who worked in the prison print shop. Even more important, the PCI print shop meant that the facility had electrical and ventilation systems capable of sustaining the type of equipment used by JBM. The print shop had the potential to become a training site for future JBM employees. One element was missing—a full-time trainer, but hiring one just for this specialized project made no economic sense. The missing link was supplied by a former JBM employee who had made a mistake that landed him in the Ohio prison system, but not at PCI. In 2016, JBM's team worked closely with PCI and the state authorities to pull all the elements together, ultimately placing the first of two paper-folding machines donated by JBM within PCI and transferring its incarcerated former team member to that facility.

Sheanshang was careful to ensure that the program treated people enrolled in the PCI program as the valued team members he hoped they would become. Participants receive a training stipend for the three to six months they are in the prerelease training program. No goods produced behind bars are sold, and any materials created are simply recycled. In addition to the former employee imprisoned at PCI, JBM supplements the training, initially sending a team lead to the facility to train inmates two to three times a week. Ashley Caudill, the HR recruiter, and Allison Rambo, the change coach, also visit PCI every one or two weeks. PCI residents who have been enrolled in JBM's training program at PCI will already have built substantial relationships with JBM's management by the time they arrive as employees. Creating a pipeline of job-ready candidates not only improved JBM's talent pipeline, but also allowed Sheanshang to offer more: "When they are trained, they can hit the ground running, and I can pay them more."

One negative about the program is that there have been some anonymous complaints that these hires are accorded preferential treatment.

Epilogue

JBM sought to solve a labor shortage. In finding the solution, the business transformed the lives of those in its Fair Chance Program, transformed the legacy employees, and, most surprising, transformed JBM itself.

That people with records who are given the chance to succeed can do so is the inspirational outcome of every true second chance company I have studied. What struck me about JBM is the way its program also changed the lives of employees. Ashley Caudill observed that the longtime employees who had been most resistant have become the most accepting, complimenting the "fair chancers" (a classification not encouraged by management, but used on the plant floor) for their old-school work ethic: "They work harder than anyone." Some employees have referred family members and neighbors into the program.

Caudill has been inspired by the experience: "I'm ready to go. . . . I love going to the prisons. . . . There are so many lives to change, so many people who need help." She is planning practical steps to move forward in her career, telling me with infectious millennial enthusiasm: "I'm super excited about this. . . . I'm going to get my master's either in social work or criminal justice." But that doesn't mean she has plans to leave JBM: "I feel honored to be part of the company for doing this."

Allison Rambo developed a twenty-week personal development curriculum dubbed The Benaiah Project. The ODRC has approved the program for use in its prisons, and participation by residents provides time credits that allow earlier release to a halfway house. Like the courage required by the biblical warrior Benaiah to face his battles, the curriculum seeks "to encourage and assist inmates in confronting and overcoming the many barriers that exist when transitioning back into society." Rambo facilitates this training for the men participating in JBM's training program at PCI and hopes that it will expand to other Ohio prisons.

Other executives changed, too. Before the Fair Chance Program, Dan Puthoff admitted, "I still maintained a fairly cold and punitive view of criminal justice." He still recalls the impact of his first visit to Nehemiah Manufacturing: "That visit did more to help me understand the concept of 'social justice' (still within the construct of capitalism) than my sixteen years of Catholic education, or perhaps sixteen years of Catholic education unknowingly prepared me for that moment when my views would change." When we spoke in June 2020, the country had witnessed mass protests spurred by the death of George Floyd's interaction with the Minneapolis police. Puthoff identifies their progress in the context of our national challenge: "How I and JBM can work to 'interrupt' racism; our work inside of the prisons provides an interesting platform to begin making a difference."

For Sheanshang, the Fair Chance Program changed his entire vision for the company: "As we learned, it really did change who we are. This was a revolution, not an evolution." The company changed its name from JBM Envelope to JBM Packaging with a broader view of its business and what the company represents. In Sheanshang's words, "We are certainly a packaging business, but we are more than that."

Most telling is the change of vision from "Dominate targeted small, open-end envelope markets" to "Be the role model for a profitable, purpose-driven company." Fair chance is now an intrinsic part of a purpose-driven company. Coupled with the new vision was a statement of purpose: "Better Solutions, Better Lives, Better World."

The change in the company's purpose flips the narrative with JBM's sales team. Where once the point was to sell more product, tied to the mission of dominating the envelope market, now

Sheanshang tells his sales group, "You have to sell a lot so we can transform more lives." The statement of purpose has focused the company on new solutions using its expertise and experience in dealing with mechanized paper-folding techniques. The company is increasingly growing its packaging business using glassine and other paper-based materials, part of the plastic-to-paper transition that is reducing plastic use worldwide. To highlight the biodegradable nature of its packaging solutions, the company trademarked the phrase, "We create packaging products with their death in mind." JBM proudly shares its Fair Chance Program with prospective customers as part of the fulfillment of its purpose. Says Sheanshang, "I want our people out there talking about this."

Linking the statements of Vision and Purpose are the six Core Values of the company. Like other companies, JBM sought to enumerate the bedrock principles to which the company should aspire, through a statement of "core values." Among the six that JBM chose is "Grit," a descriptor applied to second chance hires repeatedly in my research. Sheanshang agrees and reminds his fair chance hires that they model this value for the entire company. He also believes that their presence and the program energize the entire company, helping with recruitment and retention of traditional hires.

In the ODRC's video highlighting JBM's Fair Chance Program, Sheanshang reiterates the company's purpose-driven focus:

We're very open to helping any other business out there that might have questions. We want to promote this. We feel this is a really great opportunity. Everyone wins with it. The team member wins because they get a job, the business wins because they get an engaged team member, the community wins because we're not sending somebody back to prison.[8]

POLICIES FOR A
SECOND CHANCE AND
A THRIVING ECONOMY

When employers view people who are in prison or
otherwise touched by the criminal justice system as their
future workforce, we'll get better criminal justice policies.
—JEFF KORZENIK

It may be obvious to you that the preceding six chapters contain little in the way of government policy recommendations. There's a reason. I want to stick to my narrow area of expertise and experience. I often tell my friends active in criminal justice reform and workforce development that they work on the "supply" side of the labor market, while I'm trying to improve "demand." Criminal justice reform is incredibly complex, and even well-meaning policies have boomeranged with unintended negative consequences. Nor do I go very far into the causes of our dysfunctional and often unjust system, although I tend to be an adherent of the aphorism known as Hanlon's razor: "Never attribute to malice that which is adequately explained by stupidity."

We all agree that actions that contravene the law should have consequences, and that some of those penalties should include some combination of sanctions, fines, criminal records, community supervision, or even incarceration. Yet even if we got fair administration of the law 100 percent right, we would still have the final great miscarriage of justice—the lifelong barriers to employment faced by people who have already "paid their dues."

I shamelessly quote myself at the top of this chapter with my standard response to public questions about policy. My statement reflects a bedrock belief that employment plays a foundational role in rehabilitation and you cannot make wise policy in this arena without the employers involved. Outliers like Koch Industries have long been involved in justice policy, but its laudable efforts still cannot hope to fairly represent the concerns of American business. The past lack of widespread engagement by the business community has resulted in policies that serve neither our economy nor our communities nor the principle of justice.

Fortunately, this is changing. The demographic profile of the United States is already engaging business leaders of all political stripes in public debate and needed reform. The Society of Human Resource Management (SHRM), the trade and credentialing organization of human resource professionals, has made second chance hiring a core initiative under the "Getting Talent Back to Work" banner. The US Chamber of Commerce launched a parallel "America Moving Forward" focus. Numerous regional chambers of commerce have launched "smart justice" programs to advocate for better policy and an educated business community.

This is all very good news and is leading to long-needed criminal justice reforms, but it also comes with risks. In many cases, these policy changes will involve less supervision, whether through alternatives to incarceration, the elimination of cash bail, shortened periods of imprisonment, or lighter community supervision requirements. In other cases, restrictions may be lifted, whether for professional licensing or for driving-license suspensions. But this also means that there will be mistakes—people who might otherwise have been supervised or restricted who go on to commit new crimes. In a world where the media, particularly social media, can stir emotional responses that overwhelm logic, justice reform is vulnerable to a backlash. We need to remind ourselves that "the plural of anecdote is not data," and these instances need to be understood in a broader context.

An Employment Framework for Justice Reform

Too much of the debate is framed as a false choice between public safety and greater opportunity for people with records. Economics is the study of trade-offs, and offers a new framework for thinking about criminal justice reform. There is a common misconception that the more we loosen the restrictions on people with records, whether early release, record expungement, the elimination of cash bail or licensing restrictions, and so on, the more we will increase crime and put public safety at risk. This is, of course, a false choice. The reality is more complex, and, in a sense, more hopeful.

We need an "employment framework" for understanding public safety and the regulation of people involved in the criminal justice system. By that I mean our policy debates should incorporate the way that restrictions and supervision can be an impediment to gainful employment.

There are "win-wins" possible in criminal justice reform. More restrictions do create more public safety in a vacuum. But more restrictions also lessen public safety when they impede the ability of people to gain the employment so critical to lowered recidivism. There is a trade-off. The relationship between these opposing outcomes is conceptually illustrated in Figure 11, showing that public safety is optimized when these factors are balanced.

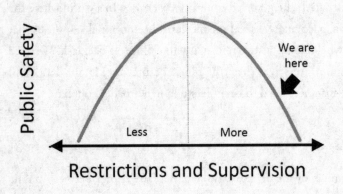

Figure 11: The Tradeoff Curve

Along this curve, I have indicated my own belief that we are at a "win-win" point, where easing restrictions would enhance public safety. This is a very broad-brush statement. There are, of course, jurisdictions where this is not true, and there are specific areas of policy where this is not the case. But, by and large, looking at the sheer volume, breadth, and indiscriminate application of the collateral sanctions, I think it is fair to say that we can do better.

Understanding the Audience:
Who Employs Whom

If the role of employment is important, then understanding the employers is critical. The recognition that sustainable employment is critical to lowering recidivism goes beyond simply acknowledging the trade-offs between restrictions, employment, and public safety. Part of improving the efficacy of our criminal justice policies is to make sure that employers participate in the formulation of the laws, regulations, and bureaucratic structures that regulate people with criminal records. Policy makers often do hear from the business community. However, to the degree companies have a voice, that of larger enterprises can be disproportionately louder. The reality is that the interests of large companies are not always the same as those of smaller firms. This can produce misguided legislation and regulation.

Companies with greater demand for labor are natural audiences for considering second chance employment, and criminal justice reform should include their perspective. In the area of employment, the perspective of small companies is particularly critical and arguably more important than that of large companies. According to 2019 data from the Bureau of Labor Statistics, nearly 60 percent of all private sector employees in the United States work for firms with fewer than a thousand employees. Looking more deeply, this employment is clustered in firms with 20 to 499 workers, which account for more than 35 percent of the American private labor force.[1]

Of course, the distribution of the labor force by size of a company tells only part of the story. A static company's labor demands are smaller than a company growing its employment—yet even here there is overlap with firms of 20 to 499 workers. A 2019 report by the Congressional Research Service summarized numerous research papers and the complexity of net job creation.[2] The oft-cited observation that new start-ups are responsible for the most job creation is true, but must be offset by the job losses that occur later as most start-ups eventually fail, with fewer than half still in business after five years. It is interesting that larger start-ups, those with 20 to 499 employees (again that category!), tend to be more significant job creators, in part because they appear to have better longevity and success.

It is unsurprising that fast-growing firms need more workers than the average, and such firms tend to be somewhat younger than their peers, no matter the size, but they are not necessarily young. There is a "barbell" effect, observed in a study of job creation in 2007, showing job creation coming from both firms in existence for five years and fewer (start-ups), but also with firms in existence for more than twenty-eight years. That study observed that the middle-aged firms (at least six years but fewer than twenty-eight) produced few net jobs.[3]

My own observations align with much of the data. "Small companies with growth needs" describes many of the employers that have pioneered or been willing to embrace second chance employment. Compared to multinationals, they have less ability to relocate facilities abroad or to other geographies with a more abundant labor supply. Their leadership also tends to be more "rooted" in the communities in which they operate, are more likely to have had personal interaction with a person with a criminal record, and are more likely to understand the broader implications for their cities and towns if more people are given the chance to rebuild their lives.

One more characteristic of employers who have created true models of second chance employment may be the most critical—they are privately owned. This has been a striking characteristic of second chance pioneers. This may be an even more important consideration than size and growth characteristics. Two of the largest, most vocal advocates for second chance hiring are privately owned corporations: Koch Industries and Virgin Group, but most pioneers are smaller and also private. Why? It is simply easier to get done in a company when the owner picks a direction or a senior executive has the ear of the owner. Even the few exceptions among public companies tend to be high-visibility, exceptional CEOs whose domains exhibit the "benevolent dictatorship" characteristics of CEO-owned companies, for example, Jamie Dimon of JPMorgan Chase.

From a policy standpoint, the good news is that privately owned and smaller-to-midsized companies are well positioned to undertake second chance hiring. The bad news is that they have distinct reason not to pursue this—hurdles that public policy makers must recognize and seek to overcome. A private business owner perceives risk as personal risk. Any financial cost is a personal cost, reputation impairment to the business is a personal affront, and something severe enough to close the business destroys not just current (and likely future) income, but net worth, and in the case of many multigenerational family-owned businesses, an entire legacy. The perceived risks associated with hiring a person with a criminal record can fall into many categories, and all are felt acutely.

It is with this backdrop that I'll lightly tread into the territory of criminal justice reform. However, I'll restrict these comments to the area where I feel I can add the value of the business perspective, which generally applies to employment-related policies. In other words, this is not intended to be a comprehensive list of reforms, but rather those that relate most directly to second chance hiring.

▶ ▶ ▶

Negligent Hiring Liability

One of the most important considerations for any hiring decision is the risk factor. Every employee creates potential risks for employers, but there is one that plays a particular role in discouraging the hiring of people with criminal records: negligent hiring liability. Employers can be exposed to liability if one of their employees causes harm to a coworker, a customer, or a third party through a job-related interaction, and that employer did not exercise reasonable due diligence in the hiring process that would have exposed such a risk.

Negligent hiring lawsuits are actually quite rare, and the data suggest that employees with a record are no more likely to cause an incident than those without a criminal history. For these reasons, many policy makers and advocates underestimate and dismiss the fears of employers. This is the wrong response. The questions that policy makers should properly consider reflect the viewpoint of employers: How costly is a negligent hiring lawsuit, and how much harder is it to defend a lawsuit if the guilty worker has a criminal record?

When reform advocates tell me that negligent hiring lawsuits hardly ever occur, my standard retort is, "I have fire insurance for my home." House fires are very rare, but they can be catastrophic, so I protect against that eventuality. Similarly, for the small and medium-sized employer, the one for whom second chance hiring is otherwise a good fit, the costs of any lawsuit can be high. Firms of this size may have limited in-house legal resources, so any lawsuit can add significantly to expenses, particularly relative to the income of a smaller operation. In these smaller firms, lawsuits can also be a huge distraction for executive management—if you are playing defense all day, you are not able to take the offensive to grow your business. Even for larger employers, this is an issue; while the legal and business cost of a lawsuit may be minimal in the overall context of a big company, it can very much be an issue for the career of a hiring manager or HR professional—no one wants to be responsible for "that hire," and face a potential cost in career trajectory, compensation, or even employment.

Fortunately, there are a number of policy fixes that not only benefit the employer through protection from negligent hiring, but also enhance the prospects of employment for people with criminal records even beyond the negligent hiring risk. Relief from negligent hiring liability falls into broad categories: restoration of rights certification, evidentiary limitation, and presumption against liability. None of these relieve the employer from the basic, commonsense, due diligence recommended in Chapter Four's process for determining suitability standards for each position—employers still have exposure if, for instance, they hire people with a history of financial fraud to handle customer funds.

The most complete protections for second chance employers from negligent hiring (and greatest benefit to job-seekers with records) are when records are expunged (completely eliminated) or sealed (not destroyed, but not visible to the public), both of which eliminate the need for a job applicant to disclose past offenses and make that history invisible to background checks of official records. In other words, employers cannot have liability tied to hiring someone with a criminal background if they could not reasonably know about the offense. Expungement has broader, positive, economic implications as well. University of Michigan Law School scholars J.J. Prescott and Sonya B. Starr examined the actual outcomes of those who went through the expungement process relative to existing trajectories. Their study concluded that this resulted in a 25 percent increase in incomes for those who won expungements through better employment outcomes, a testament to the ability of people with records to contribute to the economy if the roadblocks to hiring are cleared. These results, no doubt, have some selection bias, since the scholars found that only 6.5 percent of those eligible had gone through the expungement process, and proposed policies like automatic expungement would likely not deliver income gains as impressive, and would need to be weighed against public safety concerns.

Legal expungement or record sealing may not be as impactful without considering some kind of right-to-privacy laws. Technology entrepreneur Brian Hamilton, a longtime advocate of second chance hiring, has often observed that in the age of the internet, the closing of an official record may not be sufficient. In a *US News and World Report* opinion piece, he wrote: "In America, people who have already done their time are systematically denied a second chance due to the internet's ability to emphasize that past. . . . We cannot say Google is solely responsible for the problem of bias, but it is making discrimination significantly worse."[4] This does not negate the opportunity to broaden access to expungement and sealing, but it complicates the effectiveness.

A Certificate of Rehabilitation is a legal document granted to people with records either through an administrative process or a court. These certificates typically provide significant degrees of protection in negligent hiring cases (e.g., a criminal history unrelated to the negligent hiring charge cannot be considered), and also allow holders to earn occupational licenses that would otherwise be disallowed for people with a criminal conviction. Typically, the applicant for a Certificate of Rehabilitation has to show that he or she has taken steps to improve and is otherwise on a productive life path. From the perspective of an employer, such certificates are attractive because they not only offer liability protection, but they are an affirmation of the good character of the candidate. These certificates go by different names and offer different benefits. A state-by-state guide to these certificates as well as other paths for lowering barriers for people with records can be found in a database created by the Restoration of Rights Project. The project is a partnership of the Collateral Consequences Resource Center and several national legal associations.[5]

The most certain way to address the negligent hiring liability concerns of employers is simply to reduce or eliminate the liability completely. Under laws of "evidentiary limitation," employers cannot be held liable for an employee's criminal record if the current issue is unrelated to the nature of the past conviction. Texas goes further and provides a delineated safe harbor for second chance employers as well as landlords who rent to people with records. The employer piece (Texas Civil Practice and Remedies Code, Title 6, Section 142) includes the key clause, "The fact that the employee or independent contractor was convicted of a nonviolent, nonsexual offense before the employee or independent contractor's employment or contractual obligation with the employer, general contractor, premises owner, or other third party, as applicable, may not be introduced into evidence."

The protections for landlords are similar. Through the work of Marc Levin with the Texas Public Policy Foundation who helped draft the legislation, the language of the employer bill has been promulgated as a model policy by the American Legislative Exchange Council (ALEC) and has since been adopted by several other states.

Although generally small in number, pardons can also play a role in reducing barriers to employment. Granted by either the president or governors of individual states, pardons protect recipients from further consequences of their conviction, whether remaining terms of incarceration or most legal collateral consequences. In some states, pardons can be tied to expungement, but on their own do not eliminate or seal records, nor do they typically lessen any conviction disclosure requirements. The impact of a pardon on licensing restrictions varies from state to state, but broadly speaking, it is helpful in reducing such barriers. A 2020 study by the Economy League of Greater Philadelphia examined both the individual and aggregate impact of pardons on incomes. In Pennsylvania, pardons have far-reaching impact on disclosure and licensing and provide grounds for expungement, with benefits to both employers and prospective employees, so the economic impact in that state may be greater than average, but was quite telling. The League found that pardons filed between 2008 and 2018 resulted in an additional $16-million-plus in income with particularly dramatic impact in low income communities.[6]

Collateral Consequence Reform

Even with pardons, expungements, or sealing of records, there are simply too many institutionalized obstacles to holding a job for people with records. Collateral consequences, the penalties that go beyond any imposed by a court, have been described in this book, and for good reason. The tens of thousands of rules and regulations that restrict access to jobs, housing, and support services can effectively deny the opportunity to rebuild a life that carries the taint of a criminal record.

Restrictive occupational licensing, legal requirements to work in certain fields, is a clear and direct barrier. As always, this has to be balanced against public health and safety, and we need to be particularly vigilant in erring on the side of caution in reducing licensing restrictions designed to protect the most innocent or vulnerable: children and the infirm elderly, for example. However, as so often happens, rules developed to address narrow risks have proliferated to the point where they can do more societal harm than good. The libertarian Institute for Justice has been at the forefront in reducing licensing restrictions, not just for people with records, but broadly across the economy. The Institute has shown that nearly one in five workers today is licensed.[7] To put this in perspective, this represents a roughly fourfold increase since 1950.

Sometimes, occupational licensing specifically restricts criminal records. These are often grounded in common sense if they are narrow in their restrictions; people with a record of serious vehicular violations might appropriately be denied the licensing to be a school bus driver. The more insidious and overly broad restrictions are licenses that require "good moral character" or deny licenses based on "moral turpitude." These overly broad terms are often used to be unnecessarily restrictive. The occupation of barber is a deservedly oft-cited example. A barber's license is required in all fifty states, often requiring onerous education and application fee requirements, and typically excluding any background that includes a crime of ill-defined "moral turpitude." Although many states do offer appeal and exemption processes, that in itself becomes another barrier that discourages undertaking training in the field.

Fortunately, licensing is one area where reformers have been making significant progress. In 2015, President Barack Obama's administration issued "best practice" guidelines for state licensing,[8] and President Trump's Labor Department is making funding available for states to study their licensing laws. While licensing restrictions continue to be championed, particularly by existing holders with a vested interest in limiting competition, the momentum is clearly on the side of the reformers. The effort extends from libertarians to liberal advocacy groups like the National Employment Law Project and conservative think tanks like the Heritage Foundation among many others. To accelerate the process, the Institute for Justice has crafted model legislation, "Collateral Consequences in Occupational Licensing Act."[9]

Bail Reform

An area of recent focus has been pretrial bail reform, with reformers generally advocating for the elimination of cash bail. Traditionally, bail is a centuries-old tradition, a form of surety that the defendant will return to court when ordered and not violate the law in the intervening period. Those arrested pending trial would be released (ROR: "release on recognizance") if deemed to be neither a threat to public safety nor at risk of failing to return to the court for trial. Despite the presumption of innocence in our justice system, under certain conditions, judges may determine that defendants must be detained pending trial, typically if they have been accused of violent crimes and are considered to be a threat to public safety, were already on probation or parole at the time of arrest, or are repeat offenders. Judges may also assign conditions beyond the monetary bail amount. Within the leeway offered by the Bail Reform Act of 1984, laws vary from state to state, and there are efforts to reform practices in nearly every jurisdiction.

Traditionally, when a judge orders bail, defendants may provide the required sum of money to the court. If that is not feasible, the bail is delivered in the form of a surety bond provided by a commercial intermediary, a bail bondsman, for a nonrefundable fee, typically 10 percent of the required bail. If the defendant fails to show for trial or, in certain circumstances, commits another crime or violates pretrial release conditions, the bail becomes forfeit. Reformers argue that bail is unjust because the cost of bail has a disparate impact on the poor, resulting in excessive levels of incarceration for those who cannot afford bail, or the cost of the bondsman's fee. Judges generally have some leeway in setting bail, taking into account the accused's financial and employment situation, but the starting point for those decisions is often a "bail schedule," which assigns recommended levels of bail for each crime, or sets an amount that can be paid to the police post arrest in certain situations. Bail schedules or other formal guidelines likely "anchor" the actual determination of bail and limit the effective adjustment for a defendant's financial situation.

FRED KELLER: CHILD OF THE SIXTIES

Fred Keller, the founder and chairman of Cascade Engineering, has an issue with the title of this book: "I don't like the term 'second chances,' because most of these people never really had a first chance." From starting the company in 1973 with six workers, Fred has grown the firm to 1,600 employees in nine plants across four states as well as a European facility. It is one of the largest Certified B Corps in the world. Under Fred's leadership, Cascade has put more than eight hundred people through their Welfare to Career and "Returning Citizens" programs, employing hundreds of people with a criminal record.

Headquartered in Grand Rapids, Fred's example and advocacy inspired a groundswell of support in the western Michigan business community, leading that region of the country to become a center of second chance hiring. Fred is the cofounder and cochair of the Talent 2025 initiative, an organization of more than a hundred CEOs dedicated to growing employment and ensuring that employers have the talent resources they need in thirteen western Michigan counties. While there are similar organizations around the country, I know of none that stress the inclusion of marginalized populations to this degree. Fred cochairs the initiative's Returning Citizens Working Group.

Western Michigan is fortunate to have more than one leader in second chance hiring in the region. Mark Peters, CEO of nearby food manufacturer Butterball Farms, was inspired by Cascade's pioneering work, and not only emulated it in his own company but did pioneering work in his own right. Keller would ultimately support and collaborate with two initiatives created by Peters to drive second chance hiring in other companies—The Source, a provider of wraparound services to its twenty member companies, and the 30-2-2 initiative, which seeks to get thirty businesses to commit to hiring two recently incarcerated applicants and tracking their performance for two years. The program has twenty-three companies on board and has been emulated in other parts of the country. Many employers have had such success with their second chance employees that they hire far more than the minimal commitment. From 2014 to 2016, more than 1,700 people were placed through the initiative.

Fred practices what he preaches. He believes that "business is the most powerful force on earth," and shares his vision that "business has this wonderful opportunity to change the world for the better. Not because we must, but simply because we can." In a world where change is accelerating, "business is the most qualified, it's been the most successful, and it's developing the right tools and models." If one didn't know of Fred's business successes, his focus on community and compassion could be mistaken for naïve idealism, but it is ultimately rooted in pragmatism: "Business is organized and accustomed to change processes, it embraces problems as 'opportunities,' and we have a vested interest in healthy communities."

Like other companies that innovate in their hiring practices, Cascade is also a pioneer in other areas. Among their projects is a partnership with Chrysler, creating a "composite concept vehicle," one of the first cars with an all-plastic body, designed for developing countries.

Many of the second chance pioneers whom I have met have been motivated by deep religious belief. When I probed Fred for his source of inspiration and provided the example of some of the evangelical Christian CEOs, he stopped me; "I'm a child of the sixties!" He admits that his Methodist upbringing also played a part. He carries in his wallet John Wesley's admonition:

> Do all the good you can,
>
> By all the means you can,
>
> In all the ways you can,
>
> At all the times you can
>
> To all the people you can,
>
> As long as ever you can.

In public forums and in email exchanges, when I stress the business case, Fred has been known to interject, "And it's the right thing to do!" He is, of course, absolutely correct.

How does this relate to the economy? When viewed through the lens of employment, pretrial incarceration is devastating. It is an interruption from work that, for the employed, can start a downward spiral of shaky work history and causes employers to question the quality, reliability, and character of the worker. This, in itself, is a significant punishment for a system based on "innocent until proven guilty," but it also represents the loss of the economic contribution of a detained employee, and possibly the impairment of that individual's ability to contribute over a lifetime. A lesser macroeconomic factor, but certainly one that burdens the families of the accused, is the burden of posting bail, which can be seen as a weight on this group of consumers.

A study published in the *American Economic Review* in 2018, "The Effects of Pretrial Detention on Conviction, Future Crime, and Employment," highlights the economics of bail. The authors cite a 2013 study that showed fewer than a quarter of defendants were released on their own recognizance without a financial requirement, and that the average bail amount was $55,000. Their own report puts that sum in perspective; the 2018 study found that the defendants in the jurisdictions studied "earned less than $7,000 in the year prior to arrest, likely explaining why less than 50 percent of defendants are able to post bail even when it is set at $5,000 or less." The study also showed that the inability to pay bail resulted in a much higher rate of guilty pleas, something that should not be related to the financial condition of the defendant. The authors posit that this is an outcome of a loss of bargaining power, and if so, is clearly unjust.[10]

Allowing certain people pending trial to remain free appears to be one of those areas where the rewards are substantial and the costs are negligible when viewed over time. The study adjusted for factors like individual judge leniency tendencies, defendant histories, and other factors. In economics, we usually talk about trade-offs between risks (or costs) and rewards, and this trade-off would seem to be the risks to public safety versus the rewards of better employment outcomes. In the short run, the study shows that there have indeed been public safety risks: broader pretrial release does increase the likelihood that the accused will fail to appear. Even here, reformers argue, persuasively in my opinion, that many FTAs (failures to appear) are not fleeing the law; they were unable to appear for other reasons, including confusion surrounding court appearance summons. While unintentional FTAs may appear incredible to some, a redesign of summons forms and the implementation of text message reminders brought about a 36 percent reduction in FTAs in 2017 randomized controlled trials sponsored by the University of Chicago Crime Lab and Ideas42.[11]

From a public safety standpoint, the real issue is crime—and here the *American Economic Review* study delivers good news. While crime due to pretrial releases did indeed increase, it was almost exactly offset by reductions in crime after cases were adjudicated. Allowing more defendants to remain free pending trial did not increase crime over the long term. It is interesting, and addresses the point of this chapter, that when viewing reform through the lens of employment implications, the bulk of the decrease in crime appears related to better employment outcomes for those who were not cornered into guilty pleas during pretrial detention.

These conclusions do not release policy makers of their responsibility to approach the elimination of cash bail without prudent safeguards. Two contemporary (and geographically contiguous) approaches in New Jersey and New York illustrate the importance of data-based discipline and balanced policy. All reforms are not equal. Both states have largely eliminated bail (there are some exceptions for certain felonies); in New York, this meant widespread pretrial release, but in New Jersey, pretrial release was based on a risk assessment scoring system coupled with some judicial oversight. In New York, as of this writing, this has resulted in a widely noted increase in crime. Some of the New York reforms were already rolled back after just a few months and will likely create an appropriate balance, while the New Jersey program is proving to be both a public safety and economic success.[12]

Community Supervision Reform

Community supervision, the overarching term for probation and parole, has increasingly been recognized as an area ripe for reform, and another example of the type of win-win possible when the impact on employment is considered. Working within the existing system, experienced second chance employers have learned that they must make an accommodation to enable their hires to hold required meetings with parole or probation officers. Typically, this takes the form of work time flexibility or an appropriately private location at the workplace to hold that meeting.

Community supervision is not inherently a negative. I have had more than one employer, including those deeply devoted to the welfare of their employees, tell me that certain supervisions, particularly ankle bracelets, have had beneficial impact. The structure of electronic supervision promoted good job attendance and kept the wearers of these monitors from falling back into the environments that had contributed to their original crimes. Electronic monitoring, also used as an alternative to pretrial detention, is just a tool and can be misused. Reformers have cited abuses where the costs of monitoring fall on the wearer, becoming an undue economic burden that can impede the individual's financial stability needed for rehabilitation.

Parole conditions can become a minefield for the employee working under community conditions, leading to disruptions in employment. As discussed in Chapter Two, "technical violations"—missed meetings, certain travel or moving without permission/notification, fraternizing (or even marriage) with another felon, failure to pass a drug test, and so on. can lead to reincarceration even for transgressions that would not normally have criminal sanctions.

A July 2019 brief from the Pew Charitable Trusts pointed out four avenues of effective reforms. Cited directly from that brief:

▶ Tailoring supervision strategies toward behavioral change for those at the highest risk of re-offending.

▶ Providing positive incentives for people on supervision.

▶ Using administrative responses to violations.

▶ Capping or reducing jail or prison time for violations and limiting the conditions under which incarceration may be used to respond to a technical violation.[13]

The Pew recommendations are grounded in common sense and widely accepted within the criminal justice reform community. "Tailoring supervision" implies focusing more on those who are a higher risk to public safety and at times providing additional services to address the underlying causes of those risks, like addiction. At the same time, low-risk individuals could qualify for light supervision, and all can have the opportunity to lighten or shorten their supervision through appropriate behavior. The revolving door of supervision to incarceration because of minor technical violations is halted with penalties that are commensurate with the violation. The business community should embrace these reforms as well as an opportunity to lessen the burden on taxpayers, operate government more efficiently, and improve the ability of people with records to be contributing employees and citizens.

Again, when the impact of excessive supervision of employment is taken into account, the reforms that argue that "less is more" make sense. The experience of New York City is cited frequently and deservedly in showing that lessening the burdens of community supervision does not increase public safety risk. A 2017 paper from the Executive Sessions on Community Corrections of the Harvard Kennedy School highlights the achievements. From 1996 to 2016, the adult probation population in New York City, as a result of sentencing changes, declined by nearly 70 percent while simultaneously reducing rearrest rates, violent crime, incarceration rates, and prison populations. Among the reforms that led to this happy result, many low-risk offenders were allowed to check in at kiosks, rather than face the scheduling and transportation challenges of meeting face-to-face with probation officers. The cost savings also supported additional interventions and greater supervision for high-risk individuals, leading to a lower rearrest rate even for this challenging population.[14]

In-Prison Programming

If what happens prior to potential incarceration (e.g., bail reform) matters, as well as what happens after incarceration (e.g., parole reform), then surely what happens during incarceration also has significant impact on employment and reentry potential. Of all the types of programming available in prisons, one stands out as having the greatest positive impact on post-prison employment: education. The RAND Corporation, the historic think tank, has highlighted this opportunity. A 2013 RAND review and numerous follow-up studies found that inmates who were given opportunities to advance their education—no matter the starting level of educational attainment—fared better. Inmates who participated in correctional education programs had 13 percent better odds of employment and stunningly 43 percent lower odds of recidivating. When viewed as a taxpayer-funded workforce development program, the savings from lower reincarceration exceeded the cost of the educational resources fivefold.[15]

While vocational training has not historically had quite as dramatic an impact, I believe this may have been a reflection of the poor prospects for blue-collar careers with the decline of US-based manufacturing in the first decade of the 2000s. Programs designed to produce workers in the building trades met a similar fate with the collapse of the real estate market culminating in the 2007–2009 Great Recession. However, the trends of declining manufacturing and construction employment have both reversed since 2010, suggesting that the forward-looking prospects of these programs are even brighter than past experience.

While US manufacturing employment fell throughout the century's first decade, global manufacturing employment continued to increase over this period, proof that American manufacturing jobs were not replaced wholesale by technology, but rather were moved abroad. Since 2010, manufacturing employment in the United States has increased, and since 2012, the United States has even been gaining global market share for these jobs. The global health crisis of 2020 has fostered bipartisan interest in returning more of the supply chain to US manufacturers, particularly in pharmaceuticals and other medical supplies. It is striking that, even before the pandemic, there has been a growing shortage of workers in manufacturing, an opportunity for people with records. The construction trades have seen similar shortages of workers, which has resulted in a supply shortage in the housing industry just as millennials enter their home-buying years. The fact that many of these roles are trainable, pay well, are not customer-facing, and do not require the handling of money (preempting potential objections for second chance hiring) overcomes some of the objections for hiring people with records. In many of these industries, second chance hiring has already started to gain some traction, suggesting that in-prison training and outreach by correctional authorities will be fruitful.

Many prisons offer some type of vocational training, but Michigan's Department of Corrections has organized its efforts in ways that appear to be particularly productive. Starting at a single location in 2016 and designed to offer a more comprehensive approach to training and reemployment, the Vocational Village system will soon be at three prisons around the state. I had the pleasure of visiting the second campus at the Parnall Correctional Facility in Jackson, Michigan. Apart from a few guards (who stayed in the background) and prison uniforms, the Village felt very much like a vibrant technical college. Under the guidance of instructors with extensive private sector experience, students were actively engaged in earning certificates in CNC machining, carpentry, masonry, auto repair, and even the preparatory and simulator elements of earning a commercial driving license. Part of the power of the Vocational Village is that it puts a very public face on the availability of trained labor and encourages a partnership with the instructors, labor unions, and employers. The Villages regularly host visitors, including business leaders, who can see the opportunity. This has led to alliances such as one announced with local utility DTE Energy (formerly Detroit Edison). DTE worked with the Villages to create a new program to meet an anticipated need for tree trimmers to protect power lines; the International Brotherhood of Electrical Workers (IBEW) helped design the training equipment and invited the graduates upon release to join the union as apprentices to continue their training.

Projections of greatest future industry employment by the Bureau of Labor Statistics and others generally point to healthcare, technology, and logistics/warehousing,[16] and many of these skills can be taught in prisons. Some of this training is offered by nonprofits. The

Last Mile, a California-based nonprofit, offers software engineering at eleven facilities in four states. At San Quentin State Prison, they have established TLM Works, a website development shop, giving their trainees an opportunity to build a portfolio of work completed for real customers.

Of course, other types of programming are available behind bars, including mental health and addiction treatment. As pointed out in earlier chapters, many people with criminal records face challenges with mental and physical health. It goes without saying that addressing these can have a real impact on the potential for post-release employment, and we all wish that everything could be done today. Recognizing limited resources, and that not everything can be implemented simultaneously, my hope is that concentrating on educational and vocational training, lowered recidivism, and smaller prison populations ultimately frees up resources for these and other approaches to criminal justice (restorative justice, etc.). Innovation and experimentation in criminal justice will all work better when we stop the revolving door of recidivism, and for that, we must prioritize improving the employment prospects of those with records.

Government as Employer, Coordinator, and Customer

The focus of this book has been to build a bridge between private sector employers and applicants with records. But private sector employers, both for-profit and nonprofit entities, are not the only employers in the United States. Based on information from the Bureau of Labor Statistics at year end 2019, outside the military, there were more than twenty-three million government jobs in the United States, and of those, roughly twenty million were state and local employees.[17]

All levels of government can, as employers, play a direct role in second chance hiring. As a practical matter, local governments have the largest role to play since they have the majority of positions (nearly fifteen million as of December 2019).[18] Local governments may be best suited to become second chance employers in other ways. The nonprofits that play such a crucial role in successful second chance hiring typically have no more than a local reach, the better to align with local governments. City and town government jobs typically also include many behind-the-scenes infrastructure jobs for which there are fewer objections to people with criminal records. Of course, many government positions will consider candidates with records, but if they do so without a pipeline of referred candidates and support services, the results are no better than with private employers.

Some municipalities understand the importance of leading by example in second chance hiring. The Chicago Transit Authority (CTA) started a second chance program in 2011 with participants receiving up to a year of training and paid work experience. While there is no guarantee of a full-time job, more than 350 of 1,000-plus participants have ultimately been hired. Originally started to provide jobs cleaning buses, the CTA quickly learned that second chance hires are capable of more; expanded opportunities now include skilled mechanical and equipment maintenance.

It is no surprise that the CTA's program structure is quite similar to the successful second chance models of private sector employers. There are minimum criteria and proof of commitment—certain criminal records disqualify candidates, applicants must come from either work-release or drug/alcohol treatment programs, and must have successfully completed a four- to six-week job-readiness certificate program. There is a pipeline from nonprofit workforce agencies who refer potential participants, and just as private sector businesses have found, more potential referrers provide more quality applicants. Currently, the CTA counts nineteen social service partners; many of them are the same nonprofits to which I have referred employers in Chicago. True to successful models elsewhere, the CTA understands that a job is not enough, and participants must remain engaged with the nonprofit that referred them.

The City of Louisville, Kentucky, has developed a two-year THRIVE Fellowship, a civic and life training program specifically for Black men ages twenty-two to twenty-six who had been convicted of misdemeanors. The initiative is privately funded by the William R. Kenan, Jr. Charitable Trust, a private foundation, but is led by Louisville's Office for Safe and Healthy Neighborhoods in coordination with other groups. The thirty-two-hour-per-week program offers participants a stipend while they participate in training for civic engagement, workforce development, and related topics. The intent of the program is not just to address the needs of the THRIVE Fellows, but also allow their visible leadership and example to change the public perception and narrative surrounding justice-involved young men.

Many city governments have opened "offices of reentry," which help coordinate and advance better outcomes for returning citizens. These offices are no better or worse than the policies they implement, so the establishment of such an office is inherently neither good nor bad. However, such offices can help in reducing barriers and coordinating services. A valuable component of such work includes acting as a "convener" of potential partners in the True Second Chance Models, and in highlighting the opportunity in hiring people with records. I've had the opportunity to work a little with two such initiatives in some of our largest cities: the Los Angeles County Fair Chance Initiative and Philadelphia's Office of Reentry Partnerships.

Of course, governments interact with the business community in many ways and can choose to incentivize second chance hiring even if they do not participate themselves. The Philadelphia Fair Chance Hiring Initiative provides wage subsidies to those employers who hire the formerly incarcerated and meet certain eligibility requirements that limit the participant pool. The Cook County Social Enterprise Procurement Ordinance, introduced in 2017, provides a 5 percent pricing advantage to certain vendors to the large county government (Cook County is the second most populous county in the country and includes the city of Chicago). Among the ways that companies can qualify is by having a workforce majority of "disadvantaged" workers, an expansively defined term that includes people with a criminal record.

One area where well-intended government policy has had limited success is in direct financial support to employers of people with records, the most prominent being the Work Opportunity Tax Credit (WOTC). Data analyzed by the RAND Corporation suggests that employers may be more open to this than actually use the credit. While studies that show low participation among employers eligible for the tax credit are dated, I continue to hear anecdotally that the problem is not the concept but an application process that is too cumbersome for many second chance employers. The 2018 RAND study specifically recommends easing the paperwork burden of the application process, although payroll companies increasingly seem to be taking this burden off of employers. A 2019 Tax Foundation paper also noted that the WOTC disproportionately benefits low-wage, labor-intensive businesses. This seems to feed the Disposable Employee Model of second chance hiring, rather than make a meaningful difference for practitioners of the True Second Chance Model promoted in this book.[19]

A Note on "Ban the Box"

Perhaps the most commonly prescribed policy for improving outcomes for people with records is "Ban the Box," which prohibits employers from asking about any criminal records on the initial application. The name of this category of legislation is taken from the "box" that people with criminal records would be asked to check on human resource forms when applying for a job. Companies are still allowed to make an offer of employment contingent on a background check. This has increasingly been adopted by state and local jurisdictions and was recently included as a requirement for most contractors with the federal government (there are some exemptions for companies that have regulatory requirements for crime-free backgrounds, for example in certain defense industry roles).

The laudable idea of "Ban the Box" is that employers will give real consideration to candidates and decide their employment worthiness independent of mistakes in their past. Two issues arise. For an employer who does not understand the support mechanisms that may be needed for people with records, hiring someone with a criminal record would fall under the Undifferentiated Model of second chance employment described in Chapter Four. This is the model in which employers find that such hires tend to be great or terrible, with little in-between, essentially someone with the desire to turn his or her life around, but not always having the tools. To the degree that "Ban the Box" encourages this form of hiring, the longer-term outcome (which has not been studied) may ultimately encourage employers to say "never again" with regard to hiring people with records, a typical result for those who follow the Undifferentiated Model.

The second and already evident issue with "Ban the Box" is that, because of a negative past experience or simply ignorance about the opportunity to hire from this demographic, some employers seem to be practicing "avoidance strategies" where "Ban the Box" has been implemented. It is telling that the clearest area where "Ban the Box" has resulted in higher employment of people with records is in the public sector, the part of the economy where a potential bad hire is less likely to impact the career or finances of the hiring managers. For private sector employers, this risk is much higher, and hiring managers and other HR personnel are much more likely to reflexively revoke any offers made contingent on a background check or to select candidates they deem less likely to have criminal records (e.g., avoiding people with long gaps of unemployment). There is also evidence to suggest that some of the criteria used in avoidance strategies are creating de facto racial discrimination in hiring. Whether or not there is an actual breach of law, this is certainly something to be morally condemned. In a country where labor growth is demographically limited and no potential talent pool can be overlooked, at a minimum this is a tactic so shortsighted as to be foolish.

The approach of my work and this book has been to make "Ban the Box" legislation irrelevant. If a checked box is not an immediate disqualification for employment, no government policy is needed. My hope is that "Ban the Box" can be used as a catalyst in the business community to understand how to make the most out of considering people with criminal records. There is urgency to this wish and a deadline created by the Fair Chance to Compete for Jobs Act of 2019, which goes into effect December 20, 2021. For one, the Act requires that the federal government itself operate under "Ban the Box" rules in employment. As mentioned earlier, civilian federal government employment is smaller than either state or local payrolls, but still numbers in the millions. The wider-reaching consequence of this Jobs Act will be in the way it impacts the private sector; for positions related to work under a contract with the federal government, contractors may not ask about criminal records until a contingent offer of employment has been made. While there are three sets of exceptions to this rule (e.g., roles where national security concerns are involved), this will drive a response.

Without the understanding that there is a right and a wrong way of second chance hiring, my fear is that the Fair Chance to Compete for Jobs Act will have the same mixed results as local and state "Ban the Box" policies. These policies can do long-lasting good if accompanied by commitment and education of successful models of second chance hiring, or they can do long-lasting harm if they encourage sourcing strategies that avoid not only people with records but others with similar demographic characteristics.

We should not pretend that such policies are "magic bullets" that instantly cure complex problems, and the proponents of such legislation cannot walk away assuming the job is done. This sounds more daunting a task than it is. The business community has an innate understanding that results only come with hard work. Tell experienced business leaders that you have a "magic bullet" and they'll walk away. Tell them that a desired outcome is possible, but it takes work, and they will roll up their sleeves.

First Step Act

Although this is not a future reform, I would be remiss if I did not talk about the First Step Act, the most comprehensive criminal justice reform legislation in decades. Signed into law by President Donald Trump on December 21, 2018, it passed in Congress with widespread bipartisan support (for example, the Senate passed the bill by a margin of 88–12). In a time of considerable interparty animosity, this was a rare display of bipartisanship, and a welcome reminder of a fundamental American belief in fairness and second chances.

The Act gets to the very purpose of incarceration and seeks to restore an appropriate balance between punishment and rehabilitation. It has a strong focus on reducing recidivism and the hope for improved employment, the key markers of rehabilitation. Although the Act only governs the federal prisons (approximately 7 percent of the nation's prison population), it can help serve as a role model and catalyst for state-level reform. The bulk of the legislation covers three initiatives: 1) correctional reform, 2) sentencing reform, and 3) reauthorizing the Second Chance Act.

Specific to reforms that impact potential employment, the Act requires the US attorney general to create risk and needs assessment tools for the Bureau of Prisons (BOP) to use in developing individualized programming, a step that should greatly improve the efficacy of the programming itself. A very important aspect in the legislation is that it requires the BOP to do individual prerelease planning that critically includes getting the types of documentation needed to function outside the prison gates and be employable: a birth certificate, a social security card, driver's license (or alternative official photo ID). The BOP is also responsible for this type of planning for prisoners sentenced to community supervision.

The First Step Act also reauthorized the Second Chance Act of 2007. That legislation created several channels for funding projects and programs to reduce recidivism and improve transitions to employment. The First Step Act continued this funding, in some cases refining the potential grants and partnerships with nonprofits, faith-based organizations, and other providers. While certain aspects of the original Second Chance Act were discontinued, the First Step Act wisely continued to fund extensive research on recidivism by the

Bureau of Justice Statistics as well as authoring new studies by the National Institute of Justice. One of the striking facets of investigating the obstacles to lowering recidivism has been the scarcity of relevant and reliable data; funding this data collection and research lays the groundwork for improved outcomes. There are many more significant changes in the Act (e.g., accelerated sentence reduction formulas, housing prisoners within drivable distances to their families) that all support rehabilitation and, by extension, enhance the potential of people leaving prison to become contributing members of the workforce and society.

On April 1, 2019, I was privileged to be invited to the White House for the 2019 Prison Reform Summit and First Step Act Celebration. President Trump stood at the podium and spoke, often passionately departing from the prepared speech that was visible on the large teleprompters in the back of the room. One sentence in particular resonated with me, as the president said, "When we say 'hire American,' we mean all Americans." Behind the podium, he shared the dais with five people who had recently been released from prison under the provisions of the First Step Act, and each was invited to speak. It was deeply moving to sit in the East Room of the White House and witness the president of the United States defer to these returning citizens, relinquishing his podium and microphone. As they added their voice to the evening's event, one by one, they were embraced by the president of the United States.

It was a gathering filled with hope and promise, but policy alone cannot solve the challenge of reentry and reintegration. With the passage of time, we have been reminded of the difficulty of the task. One of the people on the dais with the president has since been rearrested.

THE SECOND
CHANCE SOCIETY

*Over the years, many nonprofits have come to me and asked
for money, but they don't ask me for advice. I have to believe
the ability of my enterprise to solve problems is greater than the
10 percent of my bottom line that I can afford to give away.*
— MARK PETERS, *CEO of Butterball Farms, Inc.*

My hope is that, by this final chapter, you appreciate how much we have to gain from second chance hiring. Undoubtedly, you also appreciate the enormity of the task. If there are shortcuts to the reentry of people with records into the workforce, I have not found them.

The task does not need to be as daunting as it may seem. In this chapter, I will discuss two ways we can move forward, the first a challenge to the business community to take "baby steps" toward exploring second chance hiring, an initiative I have called "Bridging the Box." The other half of this chapter reflects my observation that part of our problem is cultural—all too often people with a criminal record are forever the "other," never able to move beyond their worst moment, no matter how many decades pass. Without compromising public safety, how can we become more open to seeing the essential humanity of those who have made serious mistakes? This does not necessarily imply forgiveness, but at least acceptance that most people are not beyond redemption. This is the challenge set before those people who so often define our culture—those in entertainment and the arts.

Getting Started: Bridging the Box

The interested business leader does not have to commit to second chance hiring all at once or even at all. None of the second chance pioneers highlighted in this book started with fully formed referral and support networks, yet they somehow made hiring of people with records work, even before they perfected the process. The True Second Chance Model requires a significant investment of time and money, and many businesses would prefer a more incremental approach. "Bridging the Box" is a collection of six steps that offer businesses a chance to explore this talent acquisition strategy without a long-term obligation. A business can pursue one, all, or any combination of these learning experiences and policy recommendations. There is no priority to this list; the place to start is the one that appeals most.

Low-risk hires: If you are ready to hire someone with a record but not ready to commit to a full program, don't forget that there are people who have to "check the Box" but are very low-risk, low-maintenance hires. Consider the hypothetical case of someone who made a mistake at age eighteen and has been gainfully employed and a contributing member of society for more than five years. Why wouldn't you want to consider someone like that? In fact, this type of applicant may come with the "grit" that so many admire in second chance hires, and has already achieved the life stabilization that can be a struggle for those who are closer to the date of their conviction or release. In practical terms, this may mean voluntarily removing the "Box" from applications, or making sure that an applicant with a record is not automatically discarded. Some of the "accountability" tools discussed in the chapter on implementation (Chapter Five) may be needed. Too many organizations automatically discard a checked Box and too many secondary review committees have never learned the word "yes," so executive intervention may be needed to give these candidates a fair look.

Know your felony: There's clear evidence that a felony conviction is the biggest obstacle to economic advancement and reentry, much more so than misdemeanors. Yet we often don't know what a felony really represents, and it might not be the grievous offense that is often imagined. We can rightly condemn a criminal action, but also recognize that it should not represent a lifelong barrier to employment. The book *How to Become a Federal Criminal* is a great collection of the possibilities of overreach and overcharging from our federal code.[1] If you don't want to invest the time or money in the book, the author digs out one absurdity a day from the criminal code and reveals them on his Twitter feed @CrimeADay. One of the reasons we have nineteen million people with felony convictions is that we have criminalized so many activities and incentivized overcharging.

Connect with nonprofit partners: Every region of the country has nonprofits that work with people in need of a second chance. Local American Job Centers or national organizations such as Goodwill are good places to start. Many smaller but equally effective nonprofits reside within our neighborhoods and in faith-based communities. Explore what services they offer to employers and how you might be able to partner effectively. The Society for Human Resource Management (SHRM), a nonprofit membership organization, has extensive information to help the human resource professionals in your company better understand practical aspects of second chance hiring. In addition to the "Getting Talent Back to Work" Toolkit mentioned in Chapter Five, SHRM is launching a new certification course on second chance hiring, a great opportunity for HR professionals to further their education, earn a cutting-edge credential, and gain greater comfort with second chance hiring.

Connect with second chance pioneers: One of the ways that second chance hiring has spread is through the efforts of exemplary pioneers who have shared their experience and expertise. As seen in the case study of JBM Packaging in an earlier chapter, executive visits to successful employers were transformational. A visit by Kroger CEO Rodney McMullen to 180-employee Nehemiah Manufacturing was the catalyst for introducing the grocer's admirable New Beginnings Program to a company with nearly 500,000 workers. Employers of people with records exist in every geography, but a far smaller number has embraced the process that makes the True Second Chance Model successful. If you would be willing to hop on an airplane for a conference, then be willing to take a flight to see one of the great second chance employers elsewhere in the country. I have already made introductions over the years for this type of visit to the pioneers mentioned in this book. Call first, though! I can't speak for all these business leaders, but most have been incredibly willing to share their knowledge and experience with interested companies.

Review and eliminate vendor restrictions: If you're not ready to hire but are ready to help, make sure your company isn't undermining the efforts of other second chance employers. Scrutinize any restrictions that may force your vendors to exclude people with records. Why should a company's internal restrictions apply to the vendor that provides landscaping, equipment maintenance, or food service? Many construction-related unions and employers are willing to offer people with records great careers, but are stymied because customer restrictions prevent their workers from going on-site. Many of these rules were carelessly written into company policies decades ago and may not be justified. Better yet, if you are in a position to do so and your company has diversity programs in its procurement process, consider second chance employers in the initiatives. Advocate Health Care, through one such program, selected I Have a Bean coffee roasters as the coffee supplier for three of their hospitals.

Offer amnesty: This is important. In your ranks may be an employee who has contributed to the success of you and your company, but has been forced to hide a long-ago conviction. Imagine getting a job before the age of background checks, being a great employee, and then having your employer implement a no-felon rule, or being acquired by a company that has that rule and requires checks. I know of people who've been fired in these circumstances, and I know people who live in fear. For those employers who do not have regulatory barriers to doing so, offering amnesty to longtime employees is one more step toward a truly inclusive workplace. And it is the right thing to do.

Normalizing People with Records

Just as Bridging the Box offers "baby steps" toward more inclusive hiring practices, we must also think about the incremental steps society can take to reduce the social stigma of a criminal record. Make no mistake, I do not believe that every person with a record will navigate a return to a productive and lawful life; the stigma that we must address is the myth that *none* are capable, or that a crime of the past defines the character of the person today. Reducing the stigma of a record and second chance employment are mutually reinforcing. Less prejudgment makes second chance employment more frequent, which leads to more visibly favorable outcomes for people with records, which further reduces the stigma, which in turn makes it easier to consider second chance hiring—a virtuous cycle indeed.

Acceptance of people who are "different" is a cultural issue. To a large degree, the arts (literary, visual, musical) and entertainment industries define our culture. To the degree that arts are associated with our criminal justice system, they are recognized for having therapeutic value in prison. There are numerous teaching artists who contribute to the social fabric within prisons. The Justice Arts Coalition is a clearinghouse of articles, artwork and projects of visual artists.[2] There is also a worldwide Shakespeare in Prison movement, as well as playwriting programs in correctional facilities.

It's particularly beneficial when the general public gets a chance to make a connection between artistic achievement and the incarcerated. The Marin Shakespeare Company, a nonprofit theater company, also operates the largest Shakespeare in Prison programs in the world. In a memorable lunch, I had the opportunity to speak with Marin Shakespeare's cofounder Leslie Currier as well as its artist in residence, Dameion Brown. Brown had come to know Marin Shakespeare while serving twenty-three years of a life sentence in a California prison. His only training was the prison program. After release, Marin Shakespeare cast him in the title role of *Othello*, for which he won the San Francisco Bay Area Theatre Critics Circle award for Best

Actor. Other awards followed with other roles and theater companies. Second chance doesn't mean second rate in the arts either.

Music has also played a role, both therapeutically and in humanizing people behind bars. A prison choir movement grew in the
1990s and continues to help build self-esteem and community behind bars; the therapeutic benefit of many of these music programs
is enhanced further by songwriting programs. While most of this was
hidden from the public eye, the Lifers Group, a hip-hop group
formed by inmates in an East Rahway, New Jersey, prison, achieved
fame outside the prison walls. Their album was accompanied by a
documentary film, *Lifers Group World Tour: Rahway Prison, That's
It*, which was nominated for a 1992 Grammy Award for Best Long
Form Music Video.

In 2012, the Umoja Men's Chorus, a group based in an Ohio
prison since 1993, competed in the World Choir Games in Cincinnati. The inmates were not allowed to leave the facility, so the judges
traveled to them. Equally important, reporters traveled with the
judges, and their coverage and the choir's subsequent gold medal introduced thousands, perhaps millions, of people to a new way of
looking at people behind bars. Umoja and other prison choral groups
have also released albums.

Inspired by reading *The New Jim Crow*, Michelle Alexander's in-
fluential book about mass incarceration, artist/activist Fury Young
built a new record label called Die Jim Crow. The label is dedicated
to the work of currently and formerly incarcerated musicians and records in four prisons.

The visual arts also build links between the incarcerated and the
general public. Kansas City's Kemper Museum held an exhibition
of photographs by Nick Vedros. His collection of portraits, a photo

essay titled "Faces of Change," illuminated the humanity of prisoners enrolled in the Reaching Out from Within programs in Kansas prisons.

The arts also challenge our acceptance of the status quo in criminal justice. A recent exhibition curated by the Contemporary Arts Museum Houston, "Walls Turned Sideways," seeks to illuminate issues within the criminal justice system. Most of us have already come into contact with literary works that make us question what it means to be involved in the justice system. For those of us of a certain age, a high school reading assignment of *To Kill a Mockingbird* might have been our first chance to ponder the potential for injustice in our justice system. Or perhaps it was the memorable 1962 movie adaptation, winner of three Academy Awards. A Broadway production by Alan Sorkin brought the story alive for a new generation in 2018, continuing American theater's long history of illuminating social justice issues. Theater continues to inspire understanding of the criminal justice system and build empathy for the people entwined in its grasp.

A play was the inspiration and catalyst for the creation of one of the nation's oldest and largest reentry and prison reform organizations, New York City's nonprofit The Fortune Society. In 1966, Broadway producer David Rothenberg read the script for *Fortune and Men's Eyes* written by Canadian playwright John Herbert, based on his own experience of sexual abuse while incarcerated in youth reformatories. Rothenberg went on to support the play's production off-Broadway, and then realized that more was needed. He went on to found the Fortune Society.

The theater world continues to challenge the implications of a criminal record and humanize those who may have stumbled into it. Tennessee Williams was inspired in 1938 to write a play sympathetic to an inmate hunger strike, *Not about Nightingales*, when he read newspaper accounts of prisoners who suffocated in a steam room in a Pennsylvania facility. The play was lost for decades until 1998, when it was rediscovered and premiered due to the efforts of actress Vanessa Redgrave. *Notes from the Field* by Anna Deavere Smith, *Pipeline* by Dominique Morriseau, and Lynn Notage's *Sweat*, the winner of the 2017 Pulitzer for Drama, illuminate the interplay of environment and criminal justice. The audience member who can walk out of a performance and say, "There but for the grace of God go I," is someone more open to hiring a person with a record. Works that focus, not on the path to prison, but on the climb from prison to reentry, are less well known, but just as important. *Kill Floor* by Abe Koogler and *LETTIE* by Boo Killebrew are particularly good examples. *LETTIE* illuminates the complex interplay of family, housing, faith, addiction, and the question of "readiness" to rebuild a life.

PATRICIA BARRETTO: ARTS BUSINESS VISIONARY

I first met Patricia Barretto when I was being interviewed to join the board of the Harris Theater for Music and Dance. The theater is Chicago's equivalent of the Kennedy Center in Washington, simultaneously a venue for outside organizations, home to numerous resident performance groups, and the presenter of performances of the highest international standards in music and dance. The acclaimed Harris Theater Presents Series offers inclusive programming that stretches from the English National Ballet to Bangarra Dance Theater, an Australian company that showcases Aboriginal culture through contemporary dance. It is a complex and challenging business, and Patricia was then the interim CEO on her way to becoming the permanent CEO.

My passion for second chance hiring came up. I discussed the role that theater (plays and musicals) could play in building empathy for those with records, but stated that I did not see a role for classical music and dance programming typical of the Harris. Patricia immediately challenged my statement and made an executive decision: "We can do better." She reminded me that the Harris was more than a venue, it was an employer. She committed on the spot to exploring hiring marginalized workers.

Following the model of a true second chance employer, the Harris partnered with Cara Chicago, a workforce development nonprofit, and ultimately made two hires from the pipeline. Cara also provided the wraparound support needed to sustain the employment of their graduates. But under Patricia's leadership, the theater went further.

As Patricia came to understand the obstacles faced by marginalized workers, she was determined that the theater could help in other ways. The Harris staff and board participated in a work clothing drive for Cara clients. The theater worked with Cara and others to explore career pathways in the arts, from training for the database software used by most box offices to making introductions to the local stagehands union.

Finally, Patricia understood that being a theater for the Chicago community meant the entire community, and that included people with a criminal record. Realizing that she had no personal experience with people with records, she, her husband, and their young son volunteered at St. Leonard's ministry, serving meals to people who had recently exited prison. The Harris team partnered with the Heartland Alliance, a large anti-poverty organization, to better understand how the theater could be a place of true welcome and ensure that all visitors had the opportunity to experience the joy of a live performance of the highest artistic caliber. Through the the-ater's Access ticket program, the Harris strategically provides free tickets to select performances, sometimes with private backstage tours and an opportunity to meet the artists, so that people who had been marginalized and their lives fractured could build community around positive experience and witness artistic excellence.

Tragically, Patricia died at age forty-five in March 2020 after a four-year battle with cancer, but her legacy in support of marginal-ized workers continues. The theater's new CEO, Lori Dimun, is car-rying on Patricia's work, looking for even more ways that the Harris can support this part of their Chicago community. She expressed a desire I have seen in other second chance employers, the wish that these hires could have more opportunities to grow and prosper, even if it meant losing them to other organizations. Lori shared with me that she sees the theater, a nonprofit, as a gentler environment for candidates trying to reenter the workforce, assisting through the adjustment, but eventually using their time at the Harris to build a base of skills that would take them to other jobs.

One of the few produced works written from direct experience is the short play *Hit the Body Alarm* by Brad Rouse, an experienced director who spent a year incarcerated in federal jail. Rouse, who helped me compile this list of relevant plays, also reminded me that even musicals can be vehicles for creating empathy for those incarcerated:

My former boss, Hal Prince, directed the musical version of *Kiss of the Spider Woman*, with a book by Terrence McNally and a score by Kander and Ebb. The musical is set inside an Argentine prison. Only Hal Prince could direct a musical about such a hard-hitting subject.

The songs capture the heartache and frustration of being locked up. No matter where on earth you go, a jail is a jail is a jail. The feelings are primal and universal.[3]

The play *Short Eyes* was originally written by playwright Miguel Pinero for a prison writing workshop while he was incarcerated for armed robbery. The play would eventually move to Broadway where it would be nominated for six Tony Awards and receive several distinguished awards. While the drama does not create particular empathy for people behind bars, it is a testament to the artistic talent that can be found among people with records like Pinero.

I must include the culinary arts as an important agent of change, too. Perhaps it was my own epiphany at the King's Kitchen in Charlotte, North Carolina, but when people marginalized by society prepare and serve you sustenance, they are not so marginalized to you. I've seen similar reactions in others, like the CEO of an Ohio plastics company who inquired about second chance hiring after eating a meal at EDWINS, the six-month culinary training program and French restaurant in Cleveland. It works both ways: Emma Rosenbush, the general manager at San Francisco's Cala, shared with me her view that serving sustenance to others is therapeutic for her second chance workforce—they are needed, they are taking care of others, they are appreciated. There are many restaurants like this that accomplish so much more than just serving a meal: the Homeboy Café in LAX's Terminal 4, Café Momentum in Dallas, Social OTR in Cincinnati, Delancey Street Restaurant in San Francisco, DV8 Kitchen in Lexington. Some focus on youth, some on recovering addicts, but all open the patrons' eyes to see the employees as fellow humans.

Bakery and food manufacturers that focus on true second chance employment offer opportunities to appreciate the people who provide for you. Second chance bakeries from the interstate Dave's Killer Bread to open-hire paragon Greyston to neighborhood operations like Chicago's Blue Sky Bakery—all call us to ponder the fundamental humanity of those who have made mistakes. I order my coffee from I Have a Bean roasters, and get my Bee Love honey from Sweet Beginnings in Chicago, all produced by people with records—it tastes better knowing it supports rebuilding their lives.

No discussion of culture and the prison system could be complete without mentioning author and prison reformer Piper Kerman's autobiographical account, *Orange Is the New Black*. The sympathy toward women behind bars in the book was somewhat lost in translation to the TV series, but forced viewers to see incarcerated women as human beings. Television has generally not played a constructive role in humanizing people who have committed crimes, but that may be changing, too. Amid the social unrest and racial justice concerns of the summer of 2020, television networks have been canceling series of the genre of reality cop shows. Perhaps Hollywood can do even better. Carroll Bogert, CEO of The Marshall Project, a nonprofit news organization covering criminal justice, likes to share a question raised by a formerly incarcerated friend: "You remember how, at a certain point, gay characters started popping up on TV. . . . They weren't necessarily the central character, they just happened to be gay, and they were like the friend or whatever. . . . How come you never see people who have a friend, and they're just formerly incarcerated? It's just like one of the things that could be a characteristic of someone who happens to be on a TV show." When the day comes that past incarceration just happens to be a nonconsequential trait of a supporting character on a television show, we will surely have made substantial cultural progress.

What Can You Do?

If you are a senior corporate executive or a business owner, I hope this book offers some guidance on ways your organization can explore or participate in second chance hiring. I hope it also inspires you to follow in the footsteps of some of the second chance pioneers whose stories I have shared. Our case study of JBM Packaging shows how a project that helps people be great employees while also helping them rebuild their lives can have a positive impact on a company that goes way beyond just filling a labor gap. It's business, not charity, but isn't it great when good business accomplishes so much?

If you are a nonprofit leader or director of a government agency in this space, I hope this book helps you forge stronger partnerships with the business community. You can't do this without them, and they can't do this without you.

If you are a policy maker, I hope this book highlights the importance of including the perspective of the business community in questions of criminal justice policy. Businesspeople are too often caricatured as villains in criminal justice, not as the problem-solvers and decent people that the vast majority are. The smaller, family-owned businesses like the ones highlighted in this book tend to be too busy to tweet, write op-eds, lobby, or somehow get the ear of academics or the press, yet they have much to offer in formulating just policies. It's worth listening to them, even if it means traveling to obscure towns far from the major cities.

If you are an intellectually curious member of the general public, first of all, thank you for reading this book. It can be dense and technical—I always knew that (sadly) this book's value is in its content, not any lyrical quality of my prose. The fact that you are reading this and made it to the last page speaks to your willingness and determination to learn more about this critical aspect of criminal justice. I hope that you will come away with a better understanding of the complexity involved in bringing people with records back to lives of contribution and meaning. The business community is a critical part of any solution. If you know of businesses that are true second chance employers, consider supporting them with your patronage.

Finally, if you are a person burdened with a criminal record or even currently incarcerated, know that there's a growing community of people who are willing to give you a hand up. The hard work, though, is still up to you: being coachable, facing rejection after rejection, learning new skills, being in uncomfortable situations, breaking with toxic habits—and sometimes toxic people—from your past, overcoming fears, fighting the impulses of addiction. The road back is not easy, but there are a lot of people rooting for you to succeed. I hope you do.

APPENDIX A

JBM APPLICANT SCREENING

Applicant Name:	Inmate Number:
Date of Interview:	Case Worker:
Area of Relocation:	Shift Preferred:
Position Considered For:	Potential Out Date:
Reliable Transportation?	Stable Housing?
Referral Source:	Charges:

How did you get here? What led to your incarceration?

What makes you interested in JBM/position with us?

What are your top skills and/or strengths?

Do you have work experience? Externally or internally?

☐ OPI Experience

What does success look like to you?

Who is in your circle of support? Who is a healthy member, and who is not?

What have you learned about yourself while being incarcerated?	Classes/Certifications Completed

What are your triggers? How do you cope with your triggers?

How will you live differently? What is your relapse prevention plan?

© 2020 JBM Packaging

APPENDIX B

ODRC PRESENTATION FAQS

THANK YOU SO MUCH for partnering with us to bring employment opportunities to your current institution population. We are a privately owned manufacturing plant located in Lebanon, Ohio (greater Cincinnati region). We are looking forward to our upcoming recruiting visit at your institution. Here is a list of FAQs in order to help you prepare for our time together.

What can you expect from us?
- ▶ Two representatives from our HR team with "All Access" passes will come to present and interview
- ▶ We will provide all of our own materials and handouts
- ▶ The attached PowerPoint presentation (please let us know in advance if technology is not available)

What is a typical schedule?
- ▶ First hour—group presentation and questions

▶ Second and third (if needed) hour—individual speed interviews with interested candidates (approximately ten to fifteen minutes a piece)

Who are we looking to recruit?
▶ Individuals committed to change
▶ Individuals that are within six months of release
▶ Individuals who are returning or relocating to one of the following counties: Warren, Hamilton, Clinton, Butler, Greene, Montgomery, or Clermont
▶ Individuals who are detail-oriented, quality-focused, and able to stand for long periods of time
▶ Individuals who are mechanically inclined (ideal but not necessary)
▶ See jbmjobs.com for more information on open positions and requirements

Who are we NOT able to recruit at this time?
▶ Individuals who have prior convictions involving domestic violence
▶ Individuals who have prior convictions involving sexual acts
▶ Individuals who have prior convictions involving aggravated murder
▶ Individuals who have prior convictions involving extreme violence

*Note: we do also consider candidates case by case, especially if they are referred.

What do we expect from you?
- ▶ Appropriately passed inmates based upon the given criteria
- ▶ A room large enough to comfortably seat the expected audience
- ▶ A semi-private location to conduct interviews (ideally with three chairs and a table)
- ▶ The provided PowerPoint presentation pulled up and displayed for use if possible
- ▶ A sign-in sheet

What can you expect after we leave?
- ▶ Follow-up by Ashley Caudill regarding qualified candidates with assigned case managers

APPENDIX C

FAIR CHANCE COACHING DOCUMENTS

FAIR CHANCE COACHING COMMITMENT

Team Member: _____   Hire Date: _____

Welcome to JBM Packaging!

As your **Change Coach**, I want to **CONGRATULATE** you on taking an awesome next step not only in your career but also in your own personal journey toward a better life!

At JBM, we are all committed to providing "Better Solutions," working toward **"Better Lives,"** and positively contributing to a "Better World."

Our **Fair Chance Coaching** program is one-on-one coaching time with me, designed to deliver an extremely high level of accountability, loving support, and the right system, in order for **YOU** to make empowered decisions and to take bold action toward **overcoming barriers** and **achieving the goals** that **YOU** set for your life.

Saying **"YES"** to this coaching opportunity means showing up for yourself in a completely new way, mentally, spiritually, and physically.

This is the key to achieving everything you want in addition to asking for support and being open to new ways of thinking. PLUS, being willing to be challenged to go outside your comfort zone will help you to achieve your goals that much faster.

In order for you to get the most out of the Fair Chance Coaching experience, will you agree to make the following commitments?

Your commitment to the Fair Chance Coaching Program includes the following:

- ▶ To attend all weekly coaching calls or in-person meetings on time during your scheduled time for at least six months unless otherwise determined by the coach
- ▶ To be present in our time together and free from distractions
- ▶ To be authentic, honest, and open to a new way of living
- ▶ To let me know about any personal situations that may interfere with our time together
- ▶ To let it be OK not to know all the answers
- ▶ To be willing to take risks, try new things, and stretch beyond your current understanding, even if it means that you will fail
- ▶ To give yourself permission to fail but not to give up— show *grit*
- ▶ To take *ownership* and be responsible for your own results, which includes proactively asking for support, scheduling appointments, and using available resources

▶ To be patient with yourself and just focus on the next one right thing

▶ To see every barrier as an opportunity and approach difficulties with a *growth mindset*

▶ To be willing to move from a victim to a victor

▶ To celebrate every win, achievement, and step forward (including the little ones)

My commitment to you includes the following:

▶ To believe in you and your ability to overcome

▶ To share in-depth information and knowledge with you so you can move forward

▶ To allow you to be 100 percent authentic and fully YOU

▶ To hold you accountable for the steps you commit to make

▶ To be in integrity and honesty at all times

▶ To hold high standards for you and for myself

▶ To be a safe place for you to fall and get your words out

▶ To *collaborate* and work WITH you to create *innovative* and creative action steps

▶ To approach barriers WITH you and help you to find solutions and/or resources

▶ To come alongside and help you to be the best version of yourself

▶ To encourage your *passion for a better world*

▶ To celebrate with you your every win, achievement, and step forward (*especially* the little ones)

In order to get the most out of our Fair Chance Coaching experience, I will agree to make the above commitments:

▶ Coach Name: _____

- ▶ Signature: _____
- ▶ Date: _____
- ▶ TM Name: _____
- ▶ Signature: _____
- ▶ Date: _____

JBM FAIR CHANCE "BETTER LIVES" PLAN

 ## Contact Information

TM Name:	Date:
Contact Number:	
Contact Email:	
Shift:	
Emergency Contact:	

Relapse Prevention

	Signs of Trouble	Plan of Action
Emotional Relapse		
Mental Relapse		
Physical Relapse		

Support System

	Name	Contact Info
Supportive Professional		
Supportive Peer		
Supportive Mentor		
Supportive Family Member		
Other		

Planning Ahead

	Possible Problem Scenarios	Plan of Action
1		
2		
3		

🧊 Short-term Goals

	Goal	Action Step
1		
2		
3		

🧊 Long-term Goals

	Goal	Action Step
1		
2		
3		

🧊 Office Information

TM Signature:	Date:
Change Coach Signature:	Date:

FAIR CHANCE WEEKLY CHECK-IN

Team Member:	Date:

1. On a scale of 1 to 10, how firmly planted and comfortable do you feel? Why?

2. What went well this week?

3. What could have gone better this week?

4. How did you cope with challenges this week?

5. Who did you reach out to for support and accountability this week?

6. What have you done to fill your bucket this week?

7. What "One Step" are you willing to make this week toward a "healthier" you?

_____

_____

_____

8. Who could help to hold you accountable to make this one step?

_____

_____

_____

9. What roadblocks do you anticipate getting in the way of that step?

_____

_____

_____

10. How can I help/support you this week?

_____

_____

_____

APPENDIX D

RESOURCES

THE CRIMINAL JUSTICE SYSTEM is a vast and complex topic. There are thousands of potential resources, including websites, books, and podcasts. The list of links provided below, far from exhaustive, includes resources of particular relevance as well as resources mentioned in this book. Stay tuned—this list will be updated on my website: https://www.jeffkorzenik.com.

Background Reading and Information on the Criminal Justice System

Alexandra Natapoff, *Punishment without Crime: How Our Massive Misdemeanor System Traps the Innocent and Makes America More Unequal*, New York: Basic Books, 2018.

Decarceration Nation podcast: https://decarcerationnation.com/.

John Forman Jr., *Locking Up Our Own: Crime and Punishment in Black America*, New York: Farrar, Strauss and Giroux, 2017.

John Pfaff, *Locked In: The True Causes of Mass Incarceration, and How to Achieve Real Reform*, New York: Basic Books, 2017.

National Inventory of the Collateral Consequences of Conviction, National Institute of Justice: https://nij.ojp.gov/topics/articles/national-inventory-collateral-consequences-conviction.

Prison Policy Initiative: https://www.prisonpolicy.org/.

US Bureau of Justice Statistics: https://www.bjs.gov/.

Nonprofit Partners

American Jobs Center Locator: https://www.careeronestop.org/LocalHelp
/AmericanJobCenters/american-job-centers.aspx.

Goodwill Industries Reentry Program: https://www.goodwill.org/
goodwill-for-you/services-for-formerly-incarcerated-individuals/.

Lionheart Foundation "State-by-State List of Re-Entry Programs for Prisoners":
https://lionheart.org/prison/state-by-state-listing-of-r
e-entry-programs-for-prisoners/.

Other listings of reentry programs by state:

Exoffenders: https://exoffenders.net/reentry-programs-assistance/.

Jobs for Felons Hub: https://www.jobsforfelonshub.com/reentry-programs/.

ReentryWorks.com: http://www.reentryworks.com/employment/Links.aspx.

For additional local resources, simply search for "reentry organizations" in your
geography.

Implementation Guidance

Checkr, "Getting Started with Fair Chance: Hire, Onboard and Engage" course:
https://learn.checkr.com/getting-started-with-fair-chance.

Collateral Consequences Resource Center, Restoration of Rights Project
(state-by-state guidance on relief from collateral consequences): https:
//ccresourcecenter.org/restoration/.

Dave's Killer Bread Foundation Second Chance Playbook: https://www
.dkbfoundation.org/playbook-3/.

National Employment Law Project, "A Healthcare Employer Guide to Hiring
People with Arrest and Conviction Records": https://www.nelp.org
/wp-content/uploads/NELP-Safer-Toolkit-Healthcare-Employer-Guide-
Hiring-People-with-Arrest-Conviction-Records.pdf.

SHRM Foundation, Getting Talent Back to Work Digital Toolkit: https://www
.gettingtalentbacktowork.org/.

US Equal Employment Opportunity Commission: https://www.eeoc.gov/laws
/guidance/enforcement-guidance-consideration-arrest-and-conviction
-records-employment-decisions.

Second Chance Staffing and Job Boards

70 Million Jobs: https://www.70millionjobs.com/.
Cornbread Hustle (Dallas): https://cornbreadhustle.com/.
First Step Staffing (Atlanta; Nashville; Philadelphia; Duluth, GA; California):
    https://firststepstaffing.com/.
Honest Jobs: https://honestjobs.co/.
MaineWorks (Portland): https://www.maineworks.us/.

The Arts and a Second Chance Society

Die Jim Crow records: https://www.diejimcrow.com/.
Shakespeare in Prison Network: https://shakespeare.nd.edu/service
    /shakespeare-in-prisons/.
The Justice Arts Coalition: https://thejusticeartscoalition.org/.

Second Chance Restaurants and Food Businesses

All Square (Minneapolis): https://www.allsquarempls.com/restaurant.
beelove honey and honey-infused cosmetics: https://beelovebuzz.com/.
Blue Sky Bakery & Cafe (Chicago): https://www.blue-sky-bakery.org/.
Cala (San Francisco): https://www.calarestaurant.com/.
Café Reconcile (New Orleans): https://www.cafereconcile.org/.
Delancey Street Restaurant (San Francisco): http://www
    .delanceystreetfoundation.org/enterrestaurant.php.
DV8 Kitchen (Lexington, KY): https://dv8kitchen.com/.
EDWINS Restaurant (Cleveland): https://edwinsrestaurant.org/.
Homegirl Cafe (Los Angeles): https://homeboyindustries.org/social-enterprises
    /cafe/.
Hot Chicken Takeover (Columbus, OH): https://hotchickentakeover.com/.
I Have a Bean Coffee: https://www.ihaveabean.com/.
Social OTR (Cincinnati): https://socialotr.com/.
The King's Kitchen (Charlotte, NC): https://kingskitchen.org/.

ACKNOWLEDGMENTS

GRATITUDE

I KNOW IT IS TRADITIONAL to end a book with a section called "Acknowledgments," but that word alone is not adequate. One of the blessings of working with the formerly incarcerated is that one learns not to take for granted all the many gifts I have been given—the legacy of an intact family, the opportunity for and support of education, and most of all the lessons of work and resilience that were imparted at an early age.

My gratitude, therefore, must start with my parents. My father was the first to introduce me to a person with a criminal record. He was raised in severe poverty in an urban ghetto in Hartford, Connecticut, the son of immigrants. He did the "heavy lifting" within my family, becoming the first to go to college, which he financed by enlisting in the Army Air Corps at age seventeen in World War II and then using the GI Bill to double enroll in Harvard College and Harvard Law School, finishing *summa cum laude* in four and a half years. He then got his LLM (master of laws) degree at Yale while working a graveyard shift at a factory.

My father never forgot his roots. His excuse to visit his old neighborhood was weekend "errands." Around age ten or twelve, I would accompany him, and on one of these excursions he introduced me to his friend, a junk shop owner, with whom he conversed. As we stepped away, my father remarked that his friend had been in prison. When I asked the crime, he replied, "murder, a crime of passion," but stated very simply, "he did his time," a lesson that opened the door to my research.

My mother was a World War II refugee from Germany, whose Jewish family, like many, converted to Catholicism to protect their children. Eventually, she came to the United States, but only after years of on-and-off separation from her parents. Much of her childhood was spent in the charitable care of the Catholic Church, fleeing to schools in the Netherlands, in rural England, in the Carolinas and Maryland before reuniting for good with her family. It is no coincidence that one of the most effective in-prison rehabilitation nonprofits, Reaching Out from Within, benefits prisoners by their contact with a Holocaust survivor from whom they learn lessons of resiliency. Those lessons have been an intimate part of my upbringing.

Reaching Out from Within is one of many wonderful nonprofits that have generously shared their expertise and supported my work. It was truly a joy to meet that organization's founder, SuEllen Fried, and work with board member Laird Goldsborough. Nonprofits play a vital role in moving us toward a society of second chances. The leaders of many of these organizations provided me with education, introductions, and support. I know that I'm omitting names, but among the many who have given generously of their time, made introductions, and shared knowledge and friendship are Jeff Abramowitz of JEVS, Victor Dickson and Sodiqa Williams of Safer Foundation, Brenda Palms-Barber of NLEN, Maria Kim of Cara, Bettie Kirkland of Project Return, Pastor Corey Brooks and Michael Paulsen of Project H.O.O.D., Michael Swiger at True Freedom Ministries, Patricia Egipciaco of MyRebuiltLife, Jennifer Vollen-Katz at the John Howard Association, Tim Owens of The Redemption

Project, Brian Hamilton and Michelle Fishburne of the Brian Hamilton Foundation, Carroll Bogert of The Marshall Project, Dawn Freeman of the Securus Foundation, Arte Nathan with Hope for Prisoners, and Harold Rice Jr. of CEDA. I applaud SHRM's great work in educating the human resources community about second chance hiring. My first introduction came through Nick Schacht of the SHRM Foundation, and I greatly appreciate the work and support of Johnny Taylor, CEO of SHRM.

Government figures and policy makers have also given of their time and expertise—I'm not even sure they will remember our conversations, but I do: Avivah Tevah in Philadelphia as well as the team at that city's Mentor Court led by Judge Michael Erdos, and Jennifer Ballard Croft in the Cook County State's Attorney Office.

Special thanks are due to those who educated me on policies. Joshua Hoe, the creator of the essential *Decarceration Nation* podcast and a policy analyst with Safe & Just Michigan, has been an incredible resource as have Marc Levin and John Koufos.

Friends in the investment community have played an important and unexpected role in giving me an industry platform to talk about my work: Jason Trennert of Strategas Research Partners, Don Rissmiller with the Global Interdependence Center, and Steve Smith with Brandywine Investments. Other industry colleagues offered me a great sounding board for the economic aspects of this book as well as welcome encouragement, notably Don Luskin of TrendMacro and economist Ed Yardeni. My longtime friend and mentor Bob Schulman shared his own philanthropic efforts in assisting marginalized workers, and he advocated on my behalf among key business leaders. Hugh Campbell generously created an opportunity to share my message and research on Capitol Hill. Dick Hokenson, the great "dean" of demographic studies on Wall Street, has been a one-man research department bird-dogging important studies on criminal justice that I never would have found on my own. For years, the research that led to this book was done as an extension of my professional responsibilities; my colleague Claire Rubin worked tirelessly in helping me understand and communicate the economics of second chance hiring.

Although I don't give many pages to the role of the arts, I consider them important pages, and they could not have been written without the support and insight of people in the arts community: NYC Director Brad Rouse, playwright Boo Killebrew, Marin Shakespeare's Leslie Currier as well as Marin board member Heather Liston and artist-in-residence Dameion Brown, the late Patricia Barretto of the Harris Theater for Music and Dance and the current CEO Lori Dimun, and Erica Daniels at the Victory Gardens Theater.

In the visual arts, Sarah Ross, who does such great work at Statesville Prison, has opened my eyes to the world of prison arts education and provided a welcome introduction to another prison arts educator, Jen Guillemin. Elissa Tenny, president of the School of the Art Institute of Chicago, graciously hosted one of my first big opportunities to share my work, and introduced me to then chancellor Walter Massey. Walter, whose amazing career spanned triumphs in science and business, opened doors that I could never have opened on my own in corporate America.

In the culinary arts, my gratitude must start with Bo Frowine and Jim Noble at the King's Kitchen, my first real look at the potential of the culinary arts to help those marginalized lead lives of contribution and meaning; my first meal at that terrific Charlotte restaurant changed my life. Brandon Chrostowski of EDWINS amazes and inspires, as do Emma Rosenbush at Cala, Joe Hansbauer with Social OTR, and other food-oriented social enterprises at Findlay Market.

Of course, I reserve my greatest thanks for the business leaders who continue to lead the way in creating and sharing best practices in second chance hiring. This book is really their story, and you have already read the profiles of several: Fred Keller, Dan Meyer, Jeff Brown, Lloyd Martin, Ray Dalton, Marcus Sheanshang, and the late Patricia Barretto for her arts leadership. There are so many more in business who have helped and encouraged me: Frank Sinito of Millennia Companies, Mark Peters of Butterball Farms, Genevieve Martin of Dave's Killer Bread, Joe Kenner of Greyston Bakery, Michelle Cirocco at Televerde, Pete Leonard of I Have a Bean, Tom Decker at Chicago Green Insulation, Daniel Katz of TKG Environmental Service Group, Lisa Latronico at Skender, Cheri Garcia at Cornbread Hustle, and Terry Newsome at Cap Gemini. A very special thanks goes out to Mark Holden and especially Jenny Kim at Koch Industries who have been steadfast friends, resources, connectors, and teachers along the way. I have met hundreds of business leaders who have shared their experiences with hiring people with records, shooting me the occasional email, bending my ear after a presentation, or calling me out of the blue. While I don't remember each person, I remember the lessons they taught.

Taking on a first-time author with a topic that has no precedent is a chancy proposition. I am truly fortunate to have worked with Tim Burgard and the team at HarperCollins Leadership and with Jeff Farr and his colleagues at Neuwirth. Tim and Jeff were genuinely were enthusiastic about this project, and I am grateful for their patience and wisdom.

Finally, this book simply would not have gotten written without the professional support of Tim Brandhorst, my literary attorney. Tim and the leader of his firm, Marc Lane, have been constant supporters of this project from the beginning.

To all whom I have forgotten to mention, I apologize. To those I acknowledge, but did not grasp your teachings correctly, the fault is mine and mine alone. The criminal justice system is so complex, it took the time and insights of all these good people to make this book a reality. I hope it does their efforts justice.

ENDNOTES

INTRODUCTION

1. Thomas Mayer, *Monetary Policy and the Great Inflation in the United States* (Northampton, MA.: Edward Elgar Publishing, 1999), p. 1.
2. From Sam Walton, *Made in America: My Story* (New York: Bantam Books, 1993), pp. 314–17:

   RULE 1: COMMIT to your business. Believe in it more than anybody else.

   RULE 2: SHARE your profits with all your associates, and treat them as partners.

   RULE 3: MOTIVATE your partners. Money and ownership alone aren't enough.

   RULE 4: COMMUNICATE everything you possibly can to your partners. The more they know, the more they'll understand. The more they understand, the more they'll care.

   RULE 5: APPRECIATE everything your associates do for the business.

   RULE 6: CELEBRATE your successes. Find some humor in your failures.

   RULE 7: LISTEN to everyone in your company. And figure out ways to get them talking.

   RULE 8: EXCEED your customers' expectations.

   RULE 9: CONTROL your expenses better than your competition.

   RULE 10: SWIM upstream ... Ignore the conventional wisdom. If everybody else is doing it one way, there's a good chance you can find your niche by going in exactly the opposite direction.

3.   David K. Foot, Daniel Stoffman, Boom, Bust & Echo (Toronto, Canada: McFarlane, Walter and Ross, 1996), p. 2.

CHAPTER ONE

1.   *See* US Bureau of Economic Analysis, https://www.bea.gov.
2.   Congressional Budget Office, "An Update to the Economic Outlook: 2020 to 2030," July 2020, https://www.cbo.gov/publication/56465.
3.   *See* US Bureau of Economic Analysis, https://www.bea.gov.
4.   *See* US Bureau of Labor Statistics, https://www.bls.gov.
5.   *See* US Bureau of Economic Analysis, https://www.bea.gov.
6.   *See* US Bureau of Economic Analysis, https://www.bea.gov, and US Bureau of Labor Statistics, https://www.bls.gov.
7.   I'm stating the case conservatively. Critically, this million-worker shortfall assumes no change in the labor force participation rate, because it seems reasonable to assume that those who have "aged out" of the workforce—for example, retired baby boomers—will not return en masse. While a greater proportion of those seniors work compared to previous generations, it remains a distinct minority.
8.   Peter Cappellli, "Why HR Needs to Stop Passing Over the Long-Term Unemployed," *Harvard Business Review* (August 1, 2013), https://hbr.org/2013/08/what-data-show-about-hiring-th.
9.   *See* US Bureau of Labor Statistics, https://www.bls.gov.
10.   Council of Economic Advisers, *The Underestimated Cost of the Opioid Crisis*, November 2017, https://www.whitehouse.gov/sites/whitehouse.gov/files/images/The%20Underestimated%20Cost%20of%20the%20Opioid%20Crisis.pdf.
11.   Alan B. Krueger, "Where Have All the Workers Gone? An Inquiry into the Decline of the US Labor Force Participation Rate," Brookings Institute, 2017, https://www.brookings.edu/bpea-articles/where-have-all-the-workers-gone-an-inquiry-into-the-decline-of-the-u-s-labor-force-participation-rate/.
12.   Yet we must acknowledge the impact that 10 percent-plus rates of prison records have within communities, particularly the implied breakdown in intergenerational role modeling and coaching that many of us have taken for granted. As the reader will see, businesses that recognize these challenges can adapt to them and create thriving staffing and training models.
13.   Shannon, et al., "The Growth, Scope, and Spatial Distribution of People with Felony Records in the United States, 1948–2010," and for the seventy million number, National Employment Law Project (https://www.nelp.org/publication/research-supports-fair-chance-policies/#_edn1).

14.   Anastasia Christman and Michelle Natividad Rodriguez, "Research Supports Fair Chance Policy," August 1, 2016, National Employment Law Project, https://www.nelp.org/publication/research-supports-fair-chance-policies/#_edn1.

15.   Cone Communications, *Millennial Employee Engagement Study*, 2016, https://www.conecomm.com/research-blog/2016-millennial-employee-engagement-study.

16.   Cone Communications, *Millennial CSR Study*, 2015, https://www.conecomm.com/research-blog/2015-cone-communications-millennial-csr-study.

CHAPTER TWO

1.   Personal communication quoted with permission from Toussaint Romain.

2.   Charles Puzzanchera, "Juvenile Arrests, 2017," *Juvenile Justice Statistics, National Report Series Bulletin*, August 2019, Office of Justice Programs, US Department of Justice, https://ojjdp.ojp.gov/sites/g/files/xyckuh176/files/pubs/252713.pdf.

3.   National Institute of Corrections, *Topics in Community Corrections*, Assessment Issues for Managers (Washington, DC: US Department of Justice, 2004), p. 7, https://www.uc.edu/content/dam/uc/ccjr/docs/articles/ticc04_final_complete.pdf.

4.   Eli Hager, "At Least 61,000 Nationwide Are in Prison for Minor Parole Violations," The Marshall Project, April 23, 2017, https://www.themarshallproject.org/2017/04/23/at-least-61-000-nationwide-are-in-prison-for-minor-parole-violations.

5.   Jennifer Hickes Lundquist, Devah Pager, Eiko Strader, "Does a Criminal Past Predict Worker Performance? Evidence from One of America's Largest Employers," *Social Forces*, Volume 96, Issue 3, March 2018, pp. 1039–1068, https://academic.oup.com/sf/article/96/3/1039/4802355.

6.   Ibid.

7.   "Trone Private Sector and Education Advisory Council to the ACLU, Back to Business: How Hiring Formerly Incarcerated Job Seekers Benefits Your Company," 2017, American Civil Liberties Union, https://www.aclu.org/sites/default/files/field_document/060917-trone-reportweb_0.pdf.

CHAPTER THREE

1.   Personal communication quoted with permission from Bo Frowine.

2.   Mia Armstrong and Nicole Lewis, "What Gate Money Can (and Cannot) Buy," The Marshall Project, September 10, 2019, https://www.themarshallproject.org/2019/09/10/what-gate-money-can-and-cannot-buy.

3. The Exodus Planner can be found online at https://www.exodusplanner
    .com/#.

CHAPTER FOUR

1. Quoted in Jeffrey Korzenik, "A Second Chance for the Labor Pool," LinkedIn,
    August 4, 2017, https://www.linkedin.com/pulse/second-chance-labor
    -pool-jeffrey-korzenik/.
2. Michael Chu, Brian Trelstad, and John Masko, "Nehemiah Mfg. Co.:
    Providing a Second Chance," January 2020, Harvard Business School,
    https://www.hbs.edu/faculty/Pages/item.aspx?num=57027.
3. Vivian Giang, "5 Reasons Why You Aren't Getting Qualified Hires," October
    12, 2016, *LinkedIn Talent Blog*, https://business.linkedin.com/talent
    -solutions/blog/trends-and-research/2016/5-reasons-why-you-aren-t-getting
    -quality-hires.
4. American Job Centers can be located through a zip code–based search on
    https://www.careeronestop.org/LocalHelp/AmericanJobCenters/american
    -job-centers.aspx.
5. North Lawndale Employment Network, https://www.nlen.org/.
6. Emilio J. Castilla, "Social Networks and Employee Performance in a Call
    Center," *American Journal of Sociology*, Volume 110, Number 5, March 2005,
    University of Chicago Press, https://www.jstor.org/stable/10.1086/427319
    ?seq=1.
7. Paula Dutko, Michele Ver Ploeg, and Tracey Farrigan, *Characteristics and
    Influential Factors of Food Deserts*, Economic Research Report Number 140,
    August 2012, US Department of Agriculture, https://www.ers.usda.gov
    /webdocs/publications/45014/30940_err140.pdf.
8. "Redesigning the System," Panel (including Judge Ruben Castillo), School of
    the Art Institute of Chicago, April 11, 2018, https://www.youtube.com
    /watch?v=wBvCdtZfsbY&t=3607s.

CHAPTER FIVE

1. Rachel Alex Love, "A Business and Ethical Case for Second Chance Hiring,"
    Panel, Xavier University, March 4, 2020, https://youtu.be/PGES3lkwl5I.
2. On August 19, 2019, Business Roundtable members—CEOs of large
    corporations—updated a twenty-two-year-old policy statement that defined
    the purpose of corporations as maximizing shareholder returns. The revised
    policy statement can be found at: https://opportunity.businessroundtable

.org/wp-content/uploads/2020/04/BRT-Statement-on-the-Purpose-of-a-Corporation-with-Signatures-Updated-April-2020.pdf.

3. *Deloitte Global Millennial Survey 2020*, https://www2.deloitte.com/global/en/pages/about-deloitte/articles/millennialsurvey.html.

4. Personal communication.

5. Society of Human Resource Management Foundation, *Getting Talent Back to Work Digital Toolkit*, with resources and information, available at https://www.gettingtalentbacktowork.org/.

6. Dave's Killer Break Foundation, *Second Chance Playbook*, available at https://www.dkbfoundation.org/playbook-3/.

7. Personal communication.

8. Established in 1966, the Federal Bonding Program provided Fidelity Bonds for at-risk job seekers; more information at https://bonds4jobs.com/.

9. Personal communication.

10. Checkr, "How do background check reporting requirements vary by state?" December 2019, available at https://help.checkr.com/hc/en-us/articles/360000739988-How-do-background-check-reporting-requirements-vary-by-state-.

11. Personal communication.

12. Equal Employment Opportunity Commission, "Enforcement Guidance on the Consideration of Arrest and Conviction Records in Employment Decisions under Title VII of the Civil Rights Act," Number 915.002, April 25, 2012, available at https://www.eeoc.gov/laws/guidance/arrest_conviction.cfm.

13. Personal communication.

14. "A Business and Ethical Case for Second Chance Hiring," Panel, Xavier University, March 4, 2020, https://youtu.be/PGES3lkwl5I.

15. Personal communication.

16. Personal communication.

17. Barbara Campbell, "Workforce Development Collaborative," The Dalton Foundation, May 14, 2020, https://thedaltonfoundation.org/2020/05/workforcedevelopmentcollaborative/.

18. Meredith Somers, "Why you should consider an open hiring model for your business," March 16, 2018, MIT Sloan School of Management, https://mitsloan.mit.edu/ideas-made-to-matter/why-you-should-consider-open-hiring-model-your-business.

19. From the Chain Logistics website, translated by Google Translation, https://www.chain-logistics.nl/over-ons/werken-bij/.

CHAPTER SIX

1. Michael Chu, Brian Trelstad, and John Masko, "Nehemiah Mfg. Co.: Providing a Second Chance," January 2020, Harvard Business School, https://www.hbs.edu/faculty/Pages/item.aspx?num=57027.
2. Mackenzie Bean, "50 states ranked by opioid overdose death rates," January 17, 2019, Becker's Hospital Review, https://www.beckershospitalreview.com/opioids/50-states-ranked-by-opioid-overdose-death-rates.html.
3. Personal conversation during author's June 4, 2020, visit to JBM Packaging.
4. Personal communication.
5. Ibid.
6. Personal conversation during author's June 4, 2020, visit to JBM Packaging.
7. Personal communication.
8. *ODRC Partnership with JBM Envelope Company* (three-minute video), available at https://www.youtube.com/watch?v=md9GocUPDn4.

CHAPTER SEVEN

1. US Bureau of Labor Statistics, "Distribution of private sector employment by firm size class," https://www.bls.gov/web/cewbd/table_f.txt.
2. Robert Jay Dilger, Small Business Administration and Job Creation, updated June 15, 2020, Congressional Research Service, https://fas.org/sgp/crs/misc/R41523.pdf.
3. Ibid., see endnote 43, p. 9.
4. Brian Hamilton, "No Second Chance," February 5, 2018, *U.S. News and World Report*, https://www.usnews.com/opinion/civil-wars/articles/2018-02-05/former-inmates-should-have-a-way-to-expunge-records-from-google-results.
5. The Restoration of Rights project can be found online: http://ccresourcecenter.org/restoration/.
6. Ellen Spolar, Nick Frontino, Mohona Siddique, and Christion Smith, "Pardons as an Economic Investment Strategy," Economy League of Greater Philadelphia, April 2020, http://economyleague.org/uploads/files/518454652334570386-impactofpardons-final.pdf.
7. Institute for Justice, "At What Cost: Station and National Estimates of the Economic Costs of Occupational Licensing," November 2018, https://ij.org/report/at-what-cost.
8. Department of the Treasury Office of Economic Policy, Council of Economic Advisers, and Department of Labor, "Occupational Licensing: A Framework

for Policymakers," July 2015, https://obamawhitehouse.archives.gov/sites /default/files/docs/licensing_report_final_nonembargo.pdf.

9. Institute for Justice, "Collateral Consequences in Occupational Licensing Act (CCOLA)," October 31, 2019, https://ij.org/wp-content/uploads /2019/11/10-31-2019-Model-Collateral-Consequences-in-Occupational -Licensing-Act-2.pdf.

10. Will Dobbie, Jacob Goldin, and Crystal S. Yang, "The Effects of Pretrial Detention on Conviction, Future Crime, and Employment: Evidence from Randomly Assigned Judges," *American Economic Review*, Volume 108, Number 2, February 2018, pp. 201–40, https://www.aeaweb.org /articles?id=10.1257/aer.20161503.

11. Brice Cooke, Binta Zahra Diop, Alissa Fishbane, Johnathan Hayes, Aurelie Ouss, and Anuj Shah, "Using Behavioral Science to Improve Criminal Justice Outcome: Preventing Failures to Appear in Court," University of Chicago Crime Lab, January 2018, https://www.ideas42.org/wp-content/uploads /2018/03/Using-Behavioral-Science-to-Improve-Criminal-Justice -Outcomes.pdf.

12. Rafael A. Mangual, "How New Jersey Did Bail Reform Better Than New York," *New York Post*, January 12, 2020, https://www.manhattan-institute .org/how-new-jersey-did-bail-reform-better-than-new-york; Jamiles Lartey, "New York Tried to Get Rid of Bail. Then the Backlash Came," *Politico*, April 23, 2020, https://www.politico.com/news/magazine/2020/04/23/ bail-reform-coronavirus-new-york-backlash-148299; S.P. Sullivan, "N.J.'s prison reform did not cause a spike in crime, report says. But the program is going broke," NJ.com, April 2, 2019, https://www.nj.com/politics/2019/04 /njs-bail-reform-did-not-cause-a-spike-in-crime-report-says-but -the-program-is-going-broke.html.

13. The Pew Charitable Trusts, "To Safely Cut Incarceration, States Rethink Responses to Supervision Violations," July 2019, https://www.pewtrusts.org /-/media/assets/2019/07/pspp_states_target_technical_violations_v1.pdf.

14. Michael P. Jacobson, Vincent Schiraldi, Reagan Daly, and Emily Hotez, "Less Is More: How Reducing Probation Populations Can Improve Outcomes. Program in Criminal Justice Policy and Management," Harvard Kennedy School, 2017, https://www.hks.harvard.edu/sites/default/files/centers /wiener/programs/pcj/files/less_is_more_final.pdf.

15. Lois M. Davis, Robert Bozick, Jennifer L. Steele, Jessica Saunders, and Jeremy N. V. Miles, "Evaluating the Effectiveness of Correctional Education," RAND Corporation, August 22, 2013, https://www.rand.org/pubs /research_reports/RR266.html.

16. US Bureau of Labor Statistics, "Employment Projections: Industries with the fastest growing and most rapidly declining wage and salary employment," September 4, 2019, https://www.bls.gov/emp/tables/industries-fast-grow -decline-employment.htm.

17. US Bureau of Labor Statistics, "Employment by major industry sector," https://www.bls.gov/emp/tables/employment-by-major-industry-sector .htm.

18. Ibid.

19. Priscillia Hunt, Rosanna Smart, Lisa Jonsson, Flavia Tsang, "Incentivizing Employers to Hire Ex-Offenders," RAND Corporation, https://doi.org/10 .7249/RB10003.

CHAPTER 8

1. Mike Chase, *How to Become a Federal Criminal: An Illustrated Handbook for the Aspiring Offender* (New York: Atria Books, 2019).

2. More information about the Justice Arts Coalition can be found at https:// thejusticeartscoalition.org/.

3. Personal communication.

INDEX

ABOUT THE AUTHOR

Jeff Korzenik is chief investment strategist for one of the nation's largest banks, where he is responsible for the investment strategy and allocation of more than $30 billion in assets. For more than thirty years, Jeff has been known for the clarity and originality he brings to complex issues. His writings on economics and public policy have been published by *Barron's*, *Forbes*, CNN, *Newsweek*, and numerous regional publications. A noted public speaker, Jeff is a regular guest on CNBC, Fox Business News, and Bloomberg TV, and his insights into the economy, markets, manufacturing, and the workforce are frequently cited in the financial and business press. In 2020, he was elected to the Council on Criminal Justice in recognition of his research on the intersection of the labor markets and the criminal justice system. A graduate of Princeton University, he serves on numerous nonprofit boards around the country. Jeff and his wife are residents of St. Petersburg, Florida, and Marblehead, Massachusetts.